PRESIDENTIAL POWER ON TRIAL

From *Watergate* to *All the President's Men*

William Noble

Enslow Publishers, Inc.
40 Industrial Road
Box 398
Berkeley Heights, NJ 07922
USA

http://www.enslow.com

Library of Congress Cataloging-in-Publication Data

Noble, William.
    Presidential power on trial : from Watergate to All the president's men /
        William Noble.
        p. cm. — (Famous court cases that became movies)
    Includes bibliographical references and index.
    Summary: "Examines the Watergate break-in and subsequent cover-up, including
        the conspirators, the trials of the criminals, the journalists who covered the
        case, and the inspiration for All the President's Men"—Provided by publisher.
    ISBN-13: 978-0-7660-3058-9
    ISBN-10: 0-7660-3058-X
        1. Watergate Trial, Washington, D.C., 1973—Juvenile literature. 2. Watergate
    Affair, 1972–1974—Juvenile literature. 3. Executive privilege (Government
    information)—United States—Juvenile literature. I. Title.
    KF224.W33N63 2009
    342.73'062—dc22
                                                2008030969

Printed in the United States of America

10 9 8 7 6 5 4 3 2 1

To Our Readers:
We have done our best to make sure all Internet Addresses in this book were active and
appropriate when we went to press. However, the author and the publisher have no
control over and assume no liability for the material available on those Internet sites or
on other Web sites they may link to. Any comments or suggestions can be sent by e-mail
to comments@enslow.com or to the address on the back cover.

♻ Enslow Publishers, Inc., is committed to printing our books on recycled paper. The
paper in every book contains 10% to 30% post-consumer waste (PCW). The cover
board on the outside of each book contains 100% PCW. Our goal is to do our part to help
young people and the environment too!

Illustration Credits: AP/Wide World, pp. 4, 9, 14, 18, 25, 31, 35, 47, 50, 55, 64, 73, 77, 82,
86, 109; Everett Collection, pp. 1, 38, 90, 93, 96, 99, 102.

Cover Illustrations: Courthouse logo—Artville; gavel—Digital Stock; movie still of
Dustin Hoffman and Robert Redford in *All the President's Men*—Everett Collection.

CONTENTS

The Watergate complex, which housed the Democratic National Committee office, was burglarized in 1972 in a scandal that would bring down a president.

Chapter 1

The Letter

On March 23, 1972, spectators lined up to enter the courtroom of U.S. District Court Judge John J. Sirica in Washington, D.C. It was "sentencing day" for seven men who had been convicted almost two months earlier of burglarizing, copying files, and planting eavesdropping devices in Democratic National Committee offices at the Watergate complex in northwest Washington. The case had created political ripples because of ties between the burglars and people working in the administration of Republican President Richard M. Nixon, who was getting ready to run for reelection.

The burglars' arrests nine months before had sparked questions and comments from several newspapers: a Republican president and a burglary at Democratic Party offices—was there a connection?[1]

It's got nothing to do with politics, came a stiff retort from Richard Nixon's spokesman. It was only "a third-rate burglary attempt."[2]

Six months later, the trial had been held and convictions obtained, but questions about why the men did it had not been cleared up.

For Judge John Sirica, it had been a vexing problem because he *knew* deep down that the trial had not produced the full story.[3] Who was paying these people? How were they being paid? Who had authorized the burglary?

A couple of weeks after the convictions, the U.S. Senate announced it would hold hearings on the fairness of the 1972 presidential election campaign. The Senate created a select committee, composed of Democrats and Republicans, under the chairmanship of Sam Ervin, a Harvard-trained lawyer and Democrat from North Carolina, and it would hold hearings.[4]

Now, a few minutes before 10:00 A.M., spectators settled into their seats in Judge Sirica's courtroom, having passed through metal screening detectors. A door at the side of the courtroom opened, and the seven defendants walked in and took seats at the defense table. Only one—G. Gordon Liddy, a former FBI and CIA agent and an attorney—appeared relaxed and confident.[5] The others—E. Howard Hunt, Bernard Barker, Frank Sturgis, Eugenio Martínez, Virgilio González, and James W. McCord Jr., all with some CIA background—stared straight ahead while the crowd buzz lowered.

Promptly at 10:00 A.M., Judge Sirica took his place behind the high bench so he faced both the defendants and the spectators. Three days earlier, one of the defendants, James McCord, had come to his chambers uninvited, but Sirica had sent him away. He knew any private contact between a defendant and a judge prior to sentencing could lead to a mistrial. He even considered it might be a bribery attempt, since McCord had been convicted and might be looking to receive a lesser sentence.[6]

President Nixon's spokesman described the Watergate break-in as "a third-rate burglary attempt."

But later that same day, James D. Morgan, a court probation officer, had come to see Sirica and handed over a letter. "James McCord asked me to give this to you," Morgan said.[7]

McCord was a religious man and solidly involved with his family. A retired CIA officer who had also worked for the FBI, he now ran his own security firm, and he had strong ties within the Republican Party. At the time of his arrest, he had been in charge of security at the newly formed Committee to Re-elect the President. This was the group that had been in charge of getting Richard Nixon reelected as president of the United States.

Judge Sirica had called his law clerk into the office and instructed him to find a court stenographer. He would not open McCord's letter until there were witnesses and the entire proceeding could be transcribed.

Facing the defendants and the spectators, a quiet hush falling over the courtroom, Sirica knew he had

The Watergate

A six-building complex of offices, shops, condominiums, and hotel rooms in the Foggy Bottom neighborhood of Washington, the Watergate sits on ten acres of land overlooking the Potomac River. Designed by famed Italian architect Luigi Moretti and built during the 1960s, it is one of Washington's most prestigious—and expensive—addresses. A city within a city, it has landscaped courtyards, a shopping mall, a health club, restaurants, and boutiques all linked through underground passageways.[8] At the time of the Watergate burglary in 1972, influential Republicans living at the Watergate included Attorney General John Mitchell, Secretary of Commerce Maurice Stans, Republican Senator Robert Dole, and Richard Nixon's private secretary, Rose Mary Woods. It got its name from overlooking the "gate" that regulated the flow of water from the Potomac River into the Tidal Basin at flood tide.

answers to some of those disturbing questions from two months before.

There was a "preliminary matter" to take up before Judge Sirica imposed sentences.[9] He asked his clerk to unseal the envelope that contained McCord's letter and hand it to him. The courtroom, filled to capacity with the press, the defendants, their attorneys, and the prosecutors, waited expectantly.

Accused Watergate burglar James W. McCord Jr. presented a letter to Judge Sirica that stunned the courtroom.

Slowly, in a steady voice, Judge Sirica read James McCord's letter to the courtroom. It was dated four days earlier and it began: "Certain questions have been posed to me from Your Honor. . . . "[10] McCord mentioned the recently created U.S. Senate Select Committee that would look into the fairness of the 1972 presidential election campaign. He wanted to be cooperative, he said, but he felt he was "whipsawed" by the fact there may be a lawsuit because of the burglary while he may also have to testify before the Senate Committee. If he was honest before the committee, it might go badly for him in the lawsuit.

Portraying the Burglars

Several burglars, including E. Howard Hunt and James McCord, were portrayed very briefly in the burglary scene of *All the President's Men*. And all five burglars were shown from the rear as they were arraigned the afternoon following the burglary. No others mentioned in this chapter were portrayed in person, but references to G. Gordon Liddy, E. Howard Hunt, James McCord, and Judge John Sirica were made. Actual news footage was used for the opening movie scene in which Richard Nixon arrives to give the State of the Union address to a joint session of Congress as well as his August 1972 television appearance accepting the Republican nomination for the presidency.

Then, it was almost as if McCord took a deep breath, because in the next paragraph of his letter, he pointed the finger:

> 1. There was political pressure applied to the defendants to plead guilty and remain silent. . . .
>
> 2. Perjury occurred during the trial. . . .
>
> 3. Others involved in the Watergate operation were not identified during the trial when they could have been by those testifying. . . .[11]

The courtroom was stunned. When Judge Sirica finished reading the letter, there was dead silence. Then, he postponed sentencing McCord for the moment and meted out "provisional" maximum sentences of up to ten years in prison to Hunt, Barker, Sturgis, Martínez, and González. As for G. Gordon Liddy, who, like McCord, had pled not guilty, he received a twenty-year sentence and a fine of forty thousand dollars.

Judge Sirica stood and began to walk back to his chambers, and the press rushed for the door. The defendants, eyes downcast, waited to be led to their jail cells.

The next day, March 24, 1973, *The New York Times* summed it up with a headline: "Watergate Spy Says Defendants Were Under 'Political Pressure' to Admit Guilt and Keep Silent."[12]

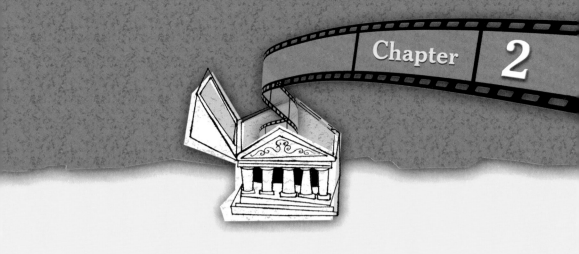

Chapter 2

The Crime

When Richard Nixon took the oath of office as president of the United States on January 20, 1969, it was a triumph of determination. Eight years earlier, he had lost the presidency to John F. Kennedy, and then, two years later, he lost an election again, this time for governor of California. Most political experts wrote him off as a loser.

But six years later, he was president of the United States. As he swept into office, he faced a major crisis: the Vietnam War, in which American soldiers had been fighting for half a decade. American casualties were in the thousands, and the cost of the war was exploding. In South Vietnam, the political situation was unstable, and the government was riddled with corruption and incompetence.

In the United States, antiwar sentiment was growing. Should preservation of South Vietnam—five thousand miles away—be crucial for protecting America? Why were Americans fighting *there* when so much needed to be done *here*? Antiwar sentiments had been heightened by two tragic events: In April 1968, famed civil rights leader Martin Luther King Jr. was assassinated in Memphis, Tennessee. Two months later, Robert F. Kennedy, brother of the late president, now running for president himself, was assassinated in Los Angeles. Both had been opposed to the Vietnam War, and both had been heroes to American young people; suddenly, they were gone!

Within weeks of Nixon's 1969 inauguration, new antiwar demonstrations broke out and continued over the next year. The president professed unconcern, even letting it be known he was watching professional football while a big antiwar demonstration took place not far from the White House.[1]

But underneath, there *was* concern, with an adviser describing the White House atmosphere as a "state of permanent crisis."[2] This led to an "us versus them" attitude, with one of Nixon's advisers saying, "You were either for us or against us, and if you were against us we were against you."[3]

In the meantime, the antiwar movement challenged Richard Nixon no matter where he traveled. Soon, the Nixon staff developed an "enemies list." It included university presidents, Hollywood personalities, political opponents, media representatives, major international organizations and foundations—several hundred names in all.[4] There were a few whom the Nixon aides really

With his wife, Pat, holding the Bible, Richard M. Nixon is sworn in as the thirty-seventh president of the United States on January 20, 1969.

disliked (such as television broadcaster Daniel Schorr, called "a real media enemy").[5] For these, active steps to offset their influence would be undertaken.

The Approaching Election

By the middle of 1970 it was time to prepare for the next presidential election, and Nixon sensed that he might not win. The Vietnam War continued to go badly, and some antiwar leaders urged a massive demonstration to shut down the United States government.[6] Moreover, the political polls showed that if the election were held just then, Nixon would have a hard time defeating Maine Senator Edmund Muskie, his expected Democratic Party challenger.[7]

H. R. Haldeman, Nixon's chief of staff (known as "Bob"), mentioned that Dwight Chapin, Nixon's appointments secretary, knew someone who could launch "dirty tricks" against their opponents, particularly Edmund Muskie, in order to even things up.[8] This would be Donald Segretti, a lawyer who, with Chapin, had played tricks on unsuspecting opponents in college elections nine to ten years earlier. The tricks included stuffing ballot boxes, passing out bogus literature, and putting spies in the other candidates' camps.[9] It had worked in college; why would it not work in a national election? Segretti would report to Chapin, and Nixon's personal lawyer, Herbert Kalmbach, would pay him from campaign funds.

Segretti got to work immediately. He crisscrossed the country more than ten times, and strange events began happening to Edmund Muskie and Democratic Party supporters. A fund-raising dinner in Washington, D.C., was thrown into chaos because unordered flowers, liquor, pizzas, Cokes, and uninvited entertainers had arrived with payment due. In New Hampshire, Democratic voters were awakened in the middle of the night and urged to vote for Muskie because he would be "so good for the black man." In Florida, a phony Muskie letter was sent around accusing named Democratic senators of unlawful sexual conduct.[10]

The Ellsberg Files

Not long after Segretti began to create his illegal mischief, another event occurred that had more lasting consequences. In the late 1960s, the Department of Defense had commissioned a no-holds-barred secret study of American involvement in Vietnam. The study was to explore how we got there, why we stayed there, and what we accomplished while we were there. The study showed that the war was unwinnable, that there would be many more casualties than publicly announced, and that no one was willing to speak out about it truthfully.[11]

Daniel Ellsberg, a Vietnam expert and Vietnam veteran, contributed to the study. He agonized as he watched his ultimate boss, Defense Secretary Robert S. McNamara, insist again and again that Vietnam victory "was just around the corner," when, in fact, the study said the opposite.[12] Quietly, Ellsberg set about photocopying the more dramatic portions of the study, and then he made the copies available to the press.

On the morning of Sunday, June 13, 1971, the headline in *The New York Times* read: "Vietnam Archive: Pentagon Study Traces 3 Decades of Growing U.S. Involvement."[13] The article gave vivid information about how the United States had been quietly involved in anticommunist military and intelligence campaigns for many years in Vietnam and neighboring countries without the American public being aware of it.

The Gulf of Tonkin Incident

The Vietnam War that Richard Nixon inherited in 1969 was the outgrowth of American policy under which U.S. troops (sixteen thousand in 1963) had been stationed in South Vietnam for some years. In 1964, North Vietnamese PT boats (small, fast patrol boats with mounted guns) attacked the USS *Maddox*, a destroyer patrolling off the coast of North Vietnam in the Gulf of Tonkin. "Under attack by three PT boats . . . " the *Maddox* radioed. American warplanes swooped in to sink or severely damage the PT boats, while the *Maddox* incurred little damage. Two days later, the USS *C. Turner Joy*, another American destroyer, reported a second attack, though many remained dubious. This was enough for President Lyndon Johnson to go on television and announce there had been "open aggression on the open seas." He ordered major air strikes on North Vietnam and asked Congress for authority "to take all necessary measures to repel any armed attack against the forces of United States and to prevent further aggression." Congress agreed overwhelmingly to what has come to be known as the "Gulf of Tonkin Resolution," and on August 7, 1964, the Vietnam "War" went into high gear.

Daniel Ellsberg, an expert on Vietnam who had worked for the Defense Department, leaked the top-secret Pentagon Papers to the press.

Within days, the published material became known as the "Pentagon Papers," and the FBI discovered that Daniel Ellsberg was the person who had leaked the papers to the newspapers. Richard Nixon was furious at what happened.

The White House filed a lawsuit to prevent further publication of the material, but the U.S. Supreme Court refused to agree. The First Amendment to the U.S. Constitution does not allow you to stop publication of something before it sees the light of day, the Court told the president two weeks after the Pentagon Papers were first published.[14]

Nixon wanted to punish Ellsberg for leaking confidential data, and he wanted to break the back of the antiwar movement, which supported Ellsberg. Nixon told his staff: "Do whatever has to be done to stop these leaks and prevent further unauthorized disclosures; I don't want to be told why it can't be done." He wanted "the most complete investigation that can be conducted." He wanted no excuses, only results.[15]

The Plumbers

A Special Investigations Unit was set up to run down leaks in the Daniel Ellsberg story as well as other leaks throughout the administration. Unit members operated out of the Executive Office Building (right across from the White House), and soon, they acquired a nickname: "Plumbers"—because their job was to stop leaks.

It did not take long for the Plumbers to zero in on Ellsberg's life. An FBI investigation of him had turned up one useful thing: He had been seeing a psychiatrist—Dr. Lewis Fielding in Los Angeles—for about two years.

The 1971 May Day Protests

As the Vietnam War dragged on, antiwar protesters wanted to send a vivid message to Richard Nixon and the U.S. government. On Monday, May 3, 1971, they planned to block major intersections and bridges leading into Washington. Thirty-five thousand protesters were camped near the Washington Monument ready to move out, but on May 2, the Nixon administration had their camping permit canceled, and local police, dressed in riot gear, moved in, fired tear gas, and broke up the encampment. About ten thousand hard-core protesters remained, and the next day, May 3, they tried to carry out their plan, only to be met by thousands of specially flown-in U.S. troops and National Guard soldiers, backing up the local police. Before it was over, seven thousand demonstrators had been arrested, making it the largest mass arrest in American history.

By now the Plumbers included E. Howard Hunt, a former CIA employee with much experience in covert (secret) activity, and G. Gordon Liddy, a lawyer and former FBI agent who reveled in a tough-guy attitude. They decided to take a look at Dr. Fielding's Ellsberg files.

Hunt recruited three Cuban exiles living in Miami (whom he had known from his CIA days), and along with Liddy, the five men flew to Los Angeles. Late in the evening of September 3, 1971, they quietly broke into Dr. Fielding's office, searched his files . . . and came away with nothing useful about Daniel Ellsberg.[16]

But a precedent had been created: The Plumbers could break the law in order to get information. In the months ahead, this would prove to be their undoing.

Plans were being made for Richard Nixon's reelection, and a special group had been set up: the Committee to Reelect the President, which came to be known by its initials, CRP (or, to its opponents, as CREEP). Nixon wanted John Mitchell, his former law partner and the current U.S. attorney general, to be CRP director, and by early 1972 that was set in place. Mitchell resigned as attorney general, and Jeb Magruder, a young White House assistant, became his chief CRP deputy.

Gemstone

On January 27, 1972, shortly before he resigned, John Mitchell held a fateful meeting. Present were John Dean, Nixon's chief lawyer; G. Gordon Liddy, now working for CRP; and Jeb Magruder. Dean had asked Liddy to prepare a political intelligence plan against the Democrats for the coming presidential campaign.[17]

Liddy arrived at the meeting well prepared. His plan, named "Gemstone," called for kidnapping antiwar demonstrators, sending spies to infiltrate Democratic campaigns, disrupting Democratic radio

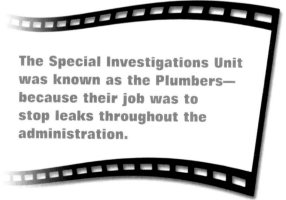

The Special Investigations Unit was known as the Plumbers—because their job was to stop leaks throughout the administration.

communications, intercepting Democratic phone calls, listening in on conversations through microphones installed in Democratic headquarters, and sabotaging the air-conditioning system during the Democratic presidential convention in hot, humid Miami.[18]

What Liddy proposed was clearly illegal, yet John Mitchell, the highest-ranking law enforcement officer in America, did not object strenuously. Liddy was asked how much it would cost. One million dollars, he responded. There was silence, and then John Mitchell said the overall plan "was not quite what [I] had in mind."[19]

At the end of the meeting, Mitchell told Liddy that his plan was too expensive. "I'd like you to . . . come back with something more realistic," he said.[20] Burn your working documents, he instructed, and that evening Liddy did so.

A week later Liddy returned with a revised, watered-down plan: Now the cost would be a half million dollars, but there would still be kidnappings, wiretaps, buggings, and spies in Democratic campaign offices. But Mitchell still would not give his okay, and Liddy became irritated and impatient.

He turned to his friend E. Howard Hunt, who had a White House office. Liddy asked him to arrange a meeting with Charles Colson, a special assistant to Nixon, who had a reputation for hardball tactics. Colson listened to Liddy, called CRP, and told Deputy Director Magruder to get on with a decision about Gemstone.[21]

Liddy had now scaled his plan down to $250,000. The more outlandish proposals, such as the kidnappings and muggings, were dropped, but wiretapping and listening in on confidential political conversations remained. On March 30, 1972, Magruder showed the plan to John Mitchell and came away with approval for an illegal break-in at Democratic National Committee (DNC) Headquarters in Washington. According to Magruder, Mitchell said of Liddy, "Ok let's give him a quarter of a million dollars and let's see what he can come up with."[22]

By now, the political landscape and reelection prospects had changed for Richard Nixon. In February, a letter quoting Edmund Muskie saying his home state of Maine had no African Americans but plenty of "Canucks" (a derogatory term for French Canadians) appeared in a New Hampshire newspaper. The paper called the letter an insult to "Franco-Americans," and it caused Muskie to lose major political support. Later, the letter was determined to be a fake, but the damage had been done.[23] In early April, Muskie was soundly beaten by George McGovern in a Democratic primary in Wisconsin, and CRP was elated. Not only did their major challenger fall, but also in George McGovern, a staunch antiwar candidate, they had an opponent they felt they could easily defeat.

With Mitchell's approval of Gemstone, the first step was to develop a team to carry out the wiretapping and bugging. Liddy recruited James McCord, chief of CRP security, for the wiretapping aspects, and Hunt went to Miami and recruited the same anti-Castro Cubans who had helped break into Dr. Lewis Fieldings's office. The Miami men were flown to Washington, where they met with McCord and learned about the plan. They would break into the Washington campaign offices of George McGovern and find what they could about Democratic plans, then break into the Watergate offices of the Democratic National Committee, install wiretaps, and photocopy documents. They were hoping to find evidence that the Democrats had received financial support from Cuba and any other people or organizations on Nixon's "enemies list."

The Break-Ins

By mid-May 1972, the team was ready. Twice, they tried to break into McGovern's headquarters after midnight, and twice they had to give up because there were staffers in the offices.

Similarly, they tried twice to break into the Watergate offices of the Democratic National Committee, and twice they had to call it off because they did not have the right lock-picking devices.

The third time at the Watergate, however, was the charm. On the evening of Sunday, May 28, 1972, a simple walkie-talkie message was relayed to E. Howard Hunt from inside DNC Headquarters: "The horse is in the house." Shortly after, Hunt called James McCord, the wiretap expert, who was waiting across the street in the Howard Johnson Motel: "My people are in; you can go in now." McCord joined the others right away and installed taps on the phone of DNC Chairman Larry O'Brien's secretary and on the phone of another staff executive. The others rifled through files and took photos of documents.[24]

Before dawn the mission was completed, and the team met in E. Howard Hunt's room for handshakes and backslaps. Across the street, at the Howard Johnson

Protesters against the war in Vietnam in Washington, D.C., in 1971. Nixon came into office during a time of growing antiwar sentiment.

Motel, a young lawyer, Alfred Baldwin, sat, earphones in hand, ready to start transcribing whatever came over the taps.

But within a week the sense of elation had dissolved. The wiretap on the phone of Larry O'Brien's secretary was not working, and the Democratic staff executive's wiretapped phone was being used, mostly, for personal calls. Also, many of the copied documents were useless. When John Mitchell read them, he barked, "This stuff isn't worth the paper it's printed on."[25]

What they needed was a tap on DNC Chairman Larry O'Brien's phone, not on his secretary's phone. So the team reassembled, and on the evening of June 16, 1972, the four Miami men, carrying two Minolta cameras for photocopying documents, checked into rooms at the Watergate Hotel. The others joined them. McCord brought three walkie-talkies, giving one to Liddy, keeping one for himself, and supplying the third to Bernard Barker, one of the Miami men. Hunt provided phony CIA identification cards and several hundred-dollar bills in case the men needed to bribe their way in or out of the offices.[26] The burglars were given cans of Mace, surgical gloves, lock-picking devices, and electronic wiretap equipment.[27]

McCord then left, took an elevator to the eighth floor, and started back down the stairs, placing a piece of tape over door latches so the corridor doors would not latch shut. He also placed tape on doors to the subbasement garage so the stairwell would be accessible from there. Then he informed Hunt and the others everything was ready.

By now it was midnight, and Watergate security guard Frank Wills began his late-night shift. From across the street, McCord could see lights in the sixth-floor Watergate DNC offices, and he cautioned Hunt and Liddy to remain patient until the offices were dark. About an hour later, Wills discovered a piece of McCord's tape on one of the garage-level doors. He removed it and continued on his rounds.

Then the lights in the DNC offices went off, and McCord walked back across the street to the Watergate Hotel. But when he and the Miami men tried to enter

What's in the Movie?

All the President's Men does not deal with events before the second Watergate break-in, so the preparation of Gemstone, the creation of the Plumbers, the break-in at Dr. Fielding's office, and the first break-in at Democratic National Committee offices do not appear in the movie. But the scene where Carl Bernstein meets with Donald Segretti and discusses Segretti's "dirty tricks" against the Democrats is accurate; Bernstein did have such a lengthy talk with Segretti, who reluctantly admitted what he had been doing. And the second break-in at DNC offices is accurately portrayed in the movie, as is the discovery of the taped stairwell door latches by security guard Frank Wills (who plays himself in the movie) and the arrest of the burglars inside the DNC offices.

through the garage stairwell and work their way to the sixth-floor DNC offices, they found the garage door latched.

So, one of the Miami men picked the lock and retaped the latch open. They climbed the stairwell to the sixth-floor offices. A short time later, security guard Wills started his second nightly security round—and found the garage door latch taped once again.

By this time McCord and the four Miami men were in the DNC offices, photocopying and picking the locks to Larry O'Brien's office.

Downstairs, Frank Wills had an uneasy feeling: the same door, taped twice within an hour—what was going on?[28]

He called the Washington, D.C., Metropolitan police. Within three minutes an unmarked police cruiser pulled up to the Watergate, and three plainclothes police officers got out. Frank Wills hailed them and showed them the taped door.

The officers told Wills to stay in the lobby and keep a watch on who might try to leave that way. Then, the police began to check each of the Watergate floors, one by one.[29]

Across the street, Alfred Baldwin watched it all unfold from the listening-post room at the Howard Johnson Motel. He could see the team inside the DNC offices, their pencil flashlights showing moving dots of light as they worked. Then, suddenly, he saw two unfamiliar shapes outlined against the office lights.

"We've got a problem," Baldwin whispered to Hunt over his walkie-talkie. Some strangers are in the DNC offices, "and they've got guns," he said. "They're looking around the balcony and everywhere, but they haven't come across our people."[30]

Within a few moments, Hunt and Liddy heard Bernard Barker's resigned voice over the walkie-talkie: "They've got us."

It was 2:30 A.M., June 17, 1972, and the Watergate drama was about to begin.[31]

Chapter 3

The Path
to Court

At 3:30 that same afternoon, federal marshals led James McCord, Bernard Barker, Eugenio Martínez, Frank Sturgis, and Virgilio González into a Washington, D.C., courtroom. After they gave their names, they were asked their occupations.

"Anti-communist," each Miami man replied.

"Security consultant," McCord responded.

When the judge asked McCord where he was a security consultant, he answered:

"CIA."[1] (Actually, he was retired from the CIA.)

That perked up courtroom interest! The police had seized several thousand dollars in hundred-dollar bills, forty rolls of unexposed film, two .75 millimeter cameras, lock picks, pen-sized tear gas guns, and elaborate wiretap and bugging devices from the burglars.

Now a CIA connection?

The police had traced the men to rooms in the Watergate Hotel, where they found an unmailed letter to a local country club with E. Howard Hunt's check inside, Bernard Barker's address book, and Eugenio Martínez's telephone directory. Both the address book and directory listed Hunt's name and phone number; alongside was the notation "W. House."

The White House?

The moment Hunt and Liddy heard Barker's words over the walkie-talkie, Hunt packed up McCord's extra electronics gear and hurried across the street to the Howard Johnson Motel. Get rid of the equipment, he told Alfred Baldwin, and get out of here. Then, Hunt went to his White House office and put McCord's electronic equipment in his safe.[2]

Liddy went to CRP and began shredding his Gemstone files. He called Jeb Magruder and was told to find Attorney General Richard Kleindienst and get James McCord released from jail immediately. Liddy tracked Kleindienst down on the golf course and admitted to him that CRP had been involved in the break-in. But Kleindienst refused to intercede for McCord, though now he knew people at CRP had broken the law.

The Cover-up Begins

By the evening after the break-in, the FBI had located E. Howard Hunt, who acknowledged that the check found at the Watergate belonged to him. But he would say nothing further without an attorney present.

E. Howard Hunt (in dark glasses) played an important role with the Plumbers. He recruited several anti-Castro Cubans to take part in the break-in at the office of Daniel Ellsberg's psychiatrist and at the Watergate.

The next day John Mitchell, as director of CRP, said, "We want to emphasize that this man [Hunt] and the other people involved were not operating on either our behalf or with our consent."[3]

Soon, Richard Nixon added his thoughts: "The White House has had no involvement whatever in this particular incident."[4]

But quietly, a cover-up was taking shape. Two days after the break-in, John Ehrlichman, Nixon's chief of domestic policy and top adviser, ordered E. Howard Hunt's White House safe opened and the contents given to John Dean, the president's lawyer. In addition to McCord's wiretap equipment in an attaché case, they found classified folders on the Pentagon Papers and on operations of the Plumbers.

"Deep six" the attaché case, Ehrlichman told Dean, adding that he should also shred the folders.[5]

Dean never did either. Several days later, he turned the material over to the acting director of the FBI, L. Patrick Gray, who went ahead and burned the files.

About the same time, Magruder retrieved his Gemstone file from CRP, and late in the evening at his home, he threw the contents into a roaring fire.

"What in the world are you doing?" his wife asked from the doorway.

"It's just some papers I have to get rid of," Magruder replied nonchalantly, as the flames consumed transcripts and photos.[6]

The Noose Begins to Tighten

By now, the FBI was tracing the hundred-dollar bills found at the Watergate Hotel. The FBI knew that banks kept records of such large bills, and slowly, the trail was leading back to CRP, where major political contributions were kept. Much of the donated money was in cash, held in finance director Maurice Stans's safe.

On June 23, 1972, six days after the burglary, Nixon met with Bob Haldeman, his chief of staff. "The FBI is not under control," Haldeman complained to Nixon. He suggested deputy CIA director Vernon Walters call L. Patrick Gray and say, "Stay the hell out of this . . .

this is business here we don't want you to go any further on it. . . . " Haldeman then quoted what he thought Gray would say to his agents: "We've got a signal from across the river [the CIA] to put a hold on this."[7]

Nixon concurred. Haldeman should have the CIA tell the FBI "'that we wish for the country, don't go any further into this case,' period!"[8]

But it simply did not work. The CIA kept insisting that it had no operation that could be damaged by the FBI investigation of the break-in.[9] And L. Patrick Gray at the FBI found himself in trouble with his own agents. "Political hack," is how one of these agents described him, and many were seething about his close ties to the White House.[10]

In addition, the prosecutors were beginning to move forward. The District of Columbia grand jury started to hear testimony on the break-in; they would decide whether crimes had been committed and who might have committed them. But John Dean, the president's lawyer, was one step ahead. He persuaded the prosecutors to allow key White House people to testify outside the presence of the grand jurors, which was highly irregular.

We do not want undue publicity about this, was Dean's argument. The prosecutors bought it—and hampered their own investigation.

By now the FBI had found G. Gordon Liddy's name in burglar Eugenio Martínez's address book, and two agents came to see him at CRP. Liddy, who was officially the lawyer for CRP's finance committee, refused to answer any questions whatsoever. When his boss

Maurice Stans heard about it, he fired him. Soon, Liddy would be added to the list of Watergate defendants.

The FBI had also traced the Watergate hundred-dollar bills to the bank account of burglar Bernard Barker in Miami. The money came, originally, from campaign contributions to the Committee to Re-elect the President, and it had been given to Barker for disbursing to the burglars.

The White House grew nervous. If the FBI could trace those hundred-dollar bills through Barker's bank account, they could waltz right into the CRP accounts. Then a link between the burglary and those around Nixon might be established.

John Dean kept pressing acting FBI Director L. Patrick Gray to slow the investigation down, so Gray directed his agents not to interview certain Republican contributors, whose money had found its way to CRP. The FBI might continue to follow the money trail, but Gray would keep his agents at the edge of the conspiracy, not in the center.

In the meantime, a young *Washington Post* reporter, Bob Woodward, had attended the arraignment of the burglars on June 17 and was intrigued by the CIA connections that came out. Later, he spoke with another *Post* reporter, Carl Bernstein, and the two began looking into the story together. At first, they uncovered a couple of minor stories, but the deeper they probed, the more complex the story became. They tracked down Hugh Sloan, assistant treasurer of CRP, and discovered that he was upset at how the campaign contributions were being used. True, Sloan had dispensed almost two hundred thousand dollars to G. Gordon Liddy (which

Reporters Carl Bernstein (left) and Bob Woodward of the *Washington Post*. Their investigation of the Watergate scandal formed the basis for the book and film *All the President's Men*.

was ultimately used in Gemstone), but he felt things were getting out of hand. In mid-July 1972, Sloan abruptly resigned from CRP, and gradually, he began to talk to Woodward and Bernstein, though he stipulated that his name could not be used as a source.

Woodward also had developed another special contact, a family friend with a high position in the government and access to information from the White House, Department of Justice, FBI, and CRP. He would not allow his name to be used, so Woodward and the *Washington Post* editors dubbed the source "Deep Throat" (after a popular X-rated movie of the time). Woodward met him at odd hours in out-of-the-way places.

From the beginning, Deep Throat had been a valuable source: He had confirmed that E. Howard Hunt was involved in Watergate and that the money in Maurice Stans's safe at CRP had financed the Watergate bugging.[11]

But Woodward and Bernstein also continued digging on their own. They had found a name—Kenneth Dahlberg—on a check for twenty-five thousand dollars that had been deposited into the bank account of Watergate burglar Bernard Barker. Tracing the name, the reporters discovered that Dahlberg was a Republican fund-raiser in the Midwest, and the check represented political contributions. How did this money get into the burglar's bank account?

"I don't have the vaguest idea," Dahlberg told Woodward. "I turn all my money over to the committee." With a little prodding, Dahlberg went further: "I turned

Deep Throat

For many years, Bob Woodward and Carl Bernstein kept the identity of Deep Throat a secret, and it was a favorite guessing game among political people in Washington. Repeated denials from "suspects" only added to mystique about the man who set up a clandestine communication system with Woodward and met him in the middle of the night to confirm the wiretapping, illegal break-ins, and money laundering schemes of the people around Richard Nixon. Then, on May 31, 2005, more than thirty years after the events, *Vanity Fair* magazine revealed the identity of Deep Throat—he was W. Mark Felt, now aged ninety-one, who had been associate director of the FBI during the Watergate years. Frail and severely ill, Felt announced that he was Deep Throat, and Bob Woodward and Carl Bernstein acknowledged him.[12]

the check over either to the treasurer of the committee [Hugh Sloan] or to Maurice Stans himself."[13]

Bingo! Here was the link between CRP and the burglary. That evening, August 1, 1972, Woodward wrote the following, which appeared the next day in the *Washington Post*: "A $25,000 cashier's check, apparently earmarked for the campaign chest of President Nixon, was deposited in April in the bank account of Bernard L. Barker, one of the five men arrested. . . . "[14]

The grand jury proceedings were heating up, too. In early July, Alfred Baldwin, the "listening post,"

W. Mark Felt, photographed in 1979. The FBI official was a confidential source for Bob Woodward, who nicknamed him "Deep Throat."

who was to transcribe what he heard over the DNC Headquarters' bug the burglars planted, decided to give himself up. He confessed his role in the burglary and implicated E. Howard Hunt and G. Gordon Liddy.

Taking Care of the Burglars

At the White House, the question of how to take care of the burglars had surfaced. Who would pay their bail, their legal expenses, and support for their families?

The Grand Jury

When a federal prosecutor thinks a serious crime has been committed and that there is enough evidence that a certain person or group is responsible, a grand jury is convened to decide whether an indictment—a list of charges that must be answered in a trial—should be issued. Grand juries, such as the Watergate grand jury at this time, were appointed for eighteen months and consisted of fifteen to twenty-three individuals who heard testimony under oath and studied documents, scientific test results, photographs, and anything else related to the crime or crimes. The prosecutor presented the evidence to the grand jury in a closed-door hearing with no other attorneys present. If the grand jury believed the evidence showed a crime had been committed and there was enough evidence that a certain person or group of people was responsible, they voted an indictment. It is at this trial that the defendants would be able to answer the charges brought against them.

Ten days after the arrests, no one had stepped forward. Finally, John Dean called Herbert Kalmbach, Nixon's West Coast lawyer and fund-raiser, and asked him to come to Washington. Dean laid it out: "We would like to have you raise funds for the legal defense of these defendants and for the support of their families."[15] There had to be "absolute secrecy"; otherwise, it could be misinterpreted and hurt the reelection campaign.

Herbert Kalmbach was not happy about the secrecy part, but the people around Nixon felt it should be done. So Kalmbach called Maurice Stans at CRP and said he needed cash. With the election less than four months away, political contributions were flowing into CRP; Stans pulled out $75,000 in hundred-dollar bills and turned the money over to Kalmbach.

The initial amount went quickly, and as the summer moved along it was followed by additional sums, totaling more than four hundred thousand dollars. But Kalmbach was beginning to have qualms about the legality of what he had been doing. He went to John Ehrlichman and asked for assurances that his passing out this money was "proper."

Yes, it is proper, Ehrlichman told him, adding that, after all, it was just for the families and their legal expenses.[16] Kalmbach was still worried, though, and a month later he resigned.

In the meantime, John Dean was able to convince acting FBI Director L. Patrick Gray to give him a heads up on whom the FBI wanted to interview. Tell us what they are looking for, Dean said. Gray went one step further; he gave Dean copies of eighty-two FBI interview reports to further prepare CRP witnesses for testifying before the

Hush Money Budget

Within a month after the Watergate break-in, plans to "take care" of the Watergate burglars were under way. A five-month budget had been prepared through CRP (which would take things safely past the 1972 presidential election), and it totaled well over $200,000, all coming from political contributions. It broke down this way: Hunt, McCord, and Liddy were each to get $3,000 per month in salary; Barker, Martínez, González, and Sturgis were to get $700 per month in "family support"; Barker was to get an additional $23,000 ($10,000 for bail, $10,000 "under the table," and $3,000 in "other expenses"); Hunt, McCord, Liddy, and Barker were each to get $25,000 to cover legal fees; Martínez, González, and Sturgis were to get $10,000 each to cover legal fees. Other miscellaneous amounts pushed the sum total even higher, and the payments were to start right away.[17]

grand jury. By now Dean was orchestrating much of the cover-up, his authority coming from the impression that he was speaking for the president. He or another White House attorney would sit in on all FBI interviews with CRP personnel, he told L. Patrick Gray, who had no objection, though some of his agents were unhappy. That unhappiness surfaced during the summer in an internal FBI report stating that some CRP personnel had asked to be interviewed away from CRP Headquarters and without CRP knowledge. "These persons advised that the presence of the [White House] attorney during the interview prevented them from being completely candid," the report concluded.[18]

The Cover-up in Full Swing

By early September 1972, the cover-up was in full swing. The president and his top aides continued to deny any knowledge of the Watergate break-in; the Watergate burglars and their families were receiving money for expenses; the FBI investigation was being "controlled"; the grand jury looking into the Watergate burglary had not uncovered the ties between the burglars and the White House (other than E. Howard Hunt); and prospects for Nixon's reelection looked promising.

Nixon's Democratic opponent, George McGovern, had not generated broad-based support. Consistently, McGovern trailed Nixon by twenty points or more in the polls, and his vehement anti–Vietnam War stance served to push him outside the mainstream— something the Nixon reelection staff emphasized at every opportunity.

But while the FBI investigation and grand jury proceedings were hampered, the activities of *Washington Post* reporters Woodward and Bernstein were not. In early September, Bernstein tracked down a CRP bookkeeper at home who admitted, "There are a lot of things that are wrong and a lot of things that are bad at [CRP]." She mentioned a "special account" at CRP where money could be extracted and no receipts issued. "You don't have to be a genius to figure it out," she said, and suddenly, Bernstein understood: The special account was actually the large chunk of cash from political contributions sitting in Maurice Stans's safe, about $350,000, from which G. Gordon Liddy had funded Gemstone.[19] This came to be called "the slush fund."

Bernstein briefed Woodward, and Woodward contacted Deep Throat. The bookkeeper had been correct, Deep Throat confirmed. That money had financed the Watergate bugging and other projects.[20]

On September 16, 1972, Woodward and Bernstein broke the story: Funds that paid for the Watergate break-in "were kept in a special account at the Committee for the Reelection of the President."[21]

The Indictments

The day before, the grand jury had handed down indictments of the burglars based on the testimony it had been hearing about the break-in throughout the summer. In addition to the five burglars, E. Howard Hunt and G. Gordon Liddy were indicted. All seven were charged with conspiracy, burglary, and violation of federal wiretapping statutes, and the case was assigned for trial after the first of the year.

Attorney General Richard Kleindienst (who had withheld Liddy's golf-course confession that CRP was involved in the break-in) trumpeted the indictments. They had resulted, he said, from "one of the most intensive, objective and thorough investigations in many years."[22]

Others were more skeptical. Who had sponsored the burglars? Why did they break in? What were they seeking? What did they hope to gain?

Woodward and Bernstein's Investigation Trail

The movie portrayed Watergate events through the eyes of *Washington Post* reporters Bob Woodward and Carl Bernstein, and their reporting did uncover major elements in the affair. The meetings between Woodward and Deep Throat actually occurred, and Deep Throat did provide information on the dirty tricks campaign, on the limits placed on the FBI investigation, on the CRP slush fund that paid for the burglaries, on Bob Haldeman's overall control of political intelligence (including the break-in itself), and on John Mitchell's prior knowledge of the break-in and other illegal acts of political espionage. "Follow the money," Deep Throat advised Woodward, and this led to the discovery of the Kenneth Dahlberg money in Bernard Barker's bank account, which Carl Bernstein actually tracked down when he went to Miami.

The meetings between Bernstein and the CRP bookkeeper are factual, and her confirmation of the slush fund and the huge amounts of money coming into CRP actually occurred.

Woodward and Bernstein's meetings with Hugh Sloan also took place, and his acknowledging the names in control of the slush fund turned out to be true.

Woodward and Bernstein went to see Hugh Sloan, the former assistant treasurer of CRP. Sloan was relaxed as they talked, even when the discussion touched on the slush fund at CRP that Woodward and Bernstein had written about a few days before. The conversation turned to John Mitchell. Did he have the power to approve spending money from the fund?

"Obviously," Sloan responded, mentioning that in all, there were five people who could approve payments from the slush fund. In addition, he said, Mitchell had known of the payments to Liddy for Gemstone.[23]

The reporters now had a big, big story: Attorney General John Mitchell, the top lawyer in America, had authorized payments to people planning illegal activities against the political opposition!

On September 29, 1972, the story ran in the *Washington Post*: "John N. Mitchell, while serving as U.S. Attorney General, personally controlled a secret Republican fund that was used to gather information about the Democrats."[24]

It was now a little more than four weeks before the election, and Richard Nixon's lead over George McGovern remained insurmountable. But as the stories of Republican wrongdoings came out during the summer and fall of 1972, the White House had reacted with a fury. The stories were "a collection of absurdities . . . a senseless pack of lies . . . shabby journalism . . . unfounded and unsubstantiated allegations . . . mud-slinging . . . " and the *Washington Post* had "maliciously sought to give the appearance of a direct connection between the White House and the Watergate."[25]

In early October 1972, Woodward met with Deep Throat to try to weave the strands of the investigation together. They had the slush fund, the tie-in between the White House and CRP, the "hush money" payments for the burglars and their families, the fierce White House opposition to the investigation, the Donald Segretti dirty tricks campaign, and the shackling of the FBI investigation, but they needed to point to a generalized plan for it all.

Woodward never revealed Deep Throat's identity to his editors, but he trusted his source and had found everything he had said to be correct. Now, Deep Throat gave him more. "I know of intelligence-gathering and games [dirty tricks] in . . . " and he named seven states and the District of Columbia. He confirmed the FBI and grand jury investigations had been limited to the Watergate affair and had not touched any other political espionage or sabotage. "None of the outside games were checked," he said, urging Woodward to look into these "other games" beyond the Watergate break-in.

It was now 3:00 A.M., and both were tired. Deep Throat stood up to leave. "It [the Canuck Letter] was a White House operation—done inside the gates surrounding the White House," he said, then he added, "You can safely say that fifty people worked for the White House and CRP to play games and spy and sabotage and gather intelligence."[26]

Then he walked off.

On October 10, 1972, Woodward and Bernstein used Deep Throat's comments to set the tone for a major story in the *Washington Post* that opened: "FBI agents have established that the Watergate bugging incident

Donald Segretti used funds from Nixon's campaign to disrupt Democratic candidates with a series of illegal "dirty tricks."

stemmed from a massive campaign of political spying and sabotage conducted on behalf of President Richard Nixon's reelection and directed by officials of the White House and the Committee for the Reelection of the President. . . . "[27]

Now the strands were coming together.

Less than a month later, however, Richard Nixon won the presidential election with more than 60 percent of the vote—a clear landslide.

Chapter 4

The Trial

The trial of the seven Watergate defendants opened in a high-ceilinged courtroom on the sixth floor of the Federal Courthouse in Washington, D.C., on the morning of January 8, 1973. E. Howard Hunt had arrived, puffing his pipe, looking pale and tense; G. Gordon Liddy had walked in smiling and waving, smoking a cigar. The four Miami men, on the other hand, stared straight ahead, their faces impassive. Reporters rushed up to James McCord throwing out questions, but he gave a terse "no comment" and continued into the courtroom.[1]

Every seat was filled. On the bench sat John J Sirica, a stern-faced jurist with seventeen years' experience.

The defendants and their attorneys sat at two tables to the judge's right, and the prosecutors, U.S. Attorney Earl Silbert and his two assistants, sat at tables on the judge's left. A large crowd of reporters was in the courtroom, along with sketch artists from the television networks.[2]

Each evening, hastily drawn images from the sketch artists would blossom on the nightly news, because the rules of the court forbade television cameras inside the courtroom. The drawings were the only way the public could get a picture of what had gone on.

The judge's clerk read the charges aloud: conspiracy, burglary, unlawful eavesdropping, and wiretapping. Then, the judge asked the defendants to stand and state whether they would plead guilty or not guilty.

"Not guilty, Your Honor," all seven said.

Two days later, after a jury had been selected, the trial began. Chief Prosecutor Earl Silbert rose and made his opening statement. For two hours he argued that there was a link between the Watergate burglary and CRP. He said that Jeb Magruder, John Mitchell's chief deputy at CRP, and others had known about the political intelligence Liddy sought to gather and that Liddy had conceived and directed the burglary. The motive behind the burglary, Silbert argued, was financial: The burglars were seeking to make themselves rich. "Certainly," Silbert concluded, "the facts will suggest . . . it was a financial motive here. . . . "[3]

Then it was the defendants' turn. Their lawyers argued that none of the defendants sought to enrich themselves through the burglary. "Why was he there?" James McCord's lawyer asked. There was no evidence

Judge John Sirica presided over the trial of the seven Watergate defendants.

that he wanted money out of this. No "financial reward or gain" was the way the lawyer put it.[4]

Hunt Pleads Guilty

A surprise occurred when court opened the next day. Behind-the-scenes discussions now led E. Howard Hunt to stand in front of the court clerk.

"Do you now wish to withdraw the plea of not guilty which was entered previously and now enter a plea of guilty?" he was asked.

"I do," Hunt replied.[5]

Suddenly, one of the architects of the Watergate burglary could not be forced to testify about White House involvement. By pleading guilty, Hunt exercised his constitutional right to say nothing more. He hoped to receive executive clemency from Richard Nixon and eventually have his guilt wiped away.

Outside the courthouse, a reporter asked Hunt whether his superiors at the White House had any connection to the Watergate burglary. "To my personal knowledge," Hunt declared, "there was none."[6]

Four days later, the burglars from Miami—Bernard Barker, Eugenio Martínez, Frank Sturgis, and Virgilio González—also asked to change their pleas to guilty.

One by one, the judge asked them: Did anyone pressure you to change this plea?

"No!" they said, "no . . . no . . . no!" vigorously shaking their heads.[7]

Where did the money come from that the police found the night of the burglary?

Executive Clemency

Under Article II, Section 2, of the U.S. Constitution, the president has the power to wipe away the guilt of a chosen few who have violated federal law by issuing "executive clemency," or a pardon for the crimes. Such clemency is not offered frequently. For example, in Richard Nixon's final year in office, he granted clemency in just 187 cases; in Bill Clinton's final day in office, January 20, 2001, he granted clemency to 140. In early 1973, E. Howard Hunt requested executive clemency as a reward for pleading guilty, and Nixon spoke with Charles Colson about it. On clemency, Nixon said, "Hunt's is a simple case. . . . " A bit later Nixon suggested they use a friendly newspaper columnist to write that Hunt "should have clemency, if you've given eighteen years of service. . . . " Except for G. Gordon Liddy, however, Nixon did not feel the same way about the other burglars. Colson put it this way: "Hunt and Liddy did the work. The others didn't know any direct information."[8]

Nixon agreed, though he never did grant executive clemency to Hunt or anyone else involved in the Watergate affair.

One by one, they denied any knowledge of that. We are American patriots, they said, we did not want George McGovern to be president.[9]

Then, the judge wondered about the cashier's check for twenty-five thousand dollars from Republican fund-raiser Kenneth Dahlberg, which the FBI had traced into Bernard Barker's account. How did Barker get that?

"Your Honor," Barker replied, "I got that money in the mail in a blank envelope."[10]

Sirica threw up his hands, looked Barker right in the eye, and told him he did not believe him.

But Sirica had no way of *disproving* what Barker said, so he accepted the Miami defendants' change of plea to guilty and deferred sentencing them until the trial ended. Now, the trial was down to just two defendants: G. Gordon Liddy and James McCord.

During the first week of the trial, the prosecutors slowly built their case, bringing witnesses to testify about the arrests at the Watergate, who was caught there, and what the police found. The prosecutors also brought witnesses who testified about Liddy's Gemstone plan to spy on George McGovern's headquarters during the campaign and to break in and plant wiretapping devices.

By the middle of the second week, the prosecution called Alfred Baldwin. He was the "listener" who had been in the Howard Johnson Motel across from the Watergate the night of the burglary and who was to transcribe the phone wiretaps placed in the DNC office. A month after the burglary, he had voluntarily given himself up to prosecutors.

Baldwin testified that he had personally delivered transcripts of wiretapped phone conversations to CRP, underscoring another link between the burglars and CRP.

The trial moved on, and by the third week the prosecution began to call CRP officials to the witness stand. Then it was the turn of Jeb Magruder, deputy director of CRP and the highest CRP official, to testify. The focus was on G. Gordon Liddy.

> One by one, the burglary defendants declared:
> We are American patriots. We did not want George McGovern to be president.

"Did you ever give Mr. Liddy any assignment concerning the Democratic National Committee?" the prosecutor asked.

"No," Magruder answered.

"Did you ever receive any report of any kind from Mr. Liddy concerning the Democratic National Committee offices. . . . ?"

"No."[11]

There was already evidence showing that Liddy had received a large sum of money from CRP for the burglary. It was certainly questionable for CRP's deputy director to claim that he did not know what Liddy did with the money.

The next witness was Hugh Sloan, former assistant treasurer of CRP. He testified that he had given money to Liddy, though he claimed not to know what the money was to be used for. By now, the judge was convinced that the full story was not going to come out, so he

Four of those involved in the Watergate break-in and cover-up (clockwise from top left): G. Gordon Liddy, counsel to the CRP; John W. Dean III, White House counsel; Jeb Stuart Magruder, deputy campaign manager for Nixon; and John N. Mitchell, U.S. attorney general.

decided to question Hugh Sloan himself. He sent the jury out of the room and asked about the money Liddy received from CRP.

"You didn't know what Mr. Liddy used it for?"

"No, sir."

"No idea?"

"No, sir."[12]

A bit later, Sirica touched on the fact that Sloan had seen Liddy at CRP the morning after the burglary. He asked what Liddy had said.

"To the best of my recollection," Sloan answered, "what he indicated was: 'My boys were caught last night. I made a mistake by using somebody from here [James McCord, CRP's security coordinator], which I told them I would never do. I am afraid I am going to lose my job.'"[13]

In all, the judge asked Sloan forty-two questions, and what he squeezed from him was to quote the admission by Liddy he had "told *them*"—meaning Liddy had been reporting to someone else.

But the prosecutors never followed up on this, and it was not the judge's job to run the prosecution. As far as the prosecutors were concerned, the entire operation had been run by Liddy and McCord with financial gain as the major reason. This was the theory the prosecutors started out with and the theory they ended with— much to Judge Sirica's dissatisfaction. The defense, meanwhile, did not put up much of a fight. Neither McCord nor Liddy took the witness stand in his own behalf. It was their right not to testify, and it could not be held against them.

On January 29, nineteen days after the trial began, it was time for final arguments to the jury. First up was the prosecutor, Earl Silbert. He went through the evidence against Liddy and McCord, step by step, emphasizing in Liddy's case that the CRP witnesses had testified Liddy had been given a lot of money. "Where did it come from?" Silbert asked the jury, adding that Liddy had been authorized to gather political intelligence and that Jeb Magruder had testified what information CRP hoped to get.

But then, the prosecutor fell back to his basic theory about financial gain. Liddy, Silbert said, "wasn't content to follow out what he was supposed to do. He had to divert it. He had to turn it." He argued that both Liddy and McCord had done the break-in for money. McCord and Liddy "were off on an enterprise of their own," Silbert concluded to the jury.[14]

When it was the defense's turn to argue to the jury, there was little they could say. Neither defendant had testified, so all their lawyers could emphasize was that both had acted for patriotic reasons. They had wanted to ensure that George McGovern would not defeat Richard

Nixon's Second Inauguration

The movie contains no scenes of the trial, nor any references to it, though it does conclude on January 20, 1973, with Richard Nixon's second presidential inauguration while the trial is in progress (the jury verdict was rendered nine days later, on January 29, 1973).

Nixon in the 1972 election. "Mr. McCord's intention was completely inconsistent with a criminal motive," McCord's lawyer argued. He "did not think he was doing anything wrong and he should not be convicted."[15]

Liddy's lawyer had an even tougher time. All he could do was question how sure other witnesses were that Liddy was the ringleader of the burglary. Perhaps, he suggested, Liddy did not know what Hunt was *really* after, and he did not know there would be wiretap devices installed. Liddy was, according to his lawyer, simply observing the burglary from across the street, not participating in it.

But, of course, that made little sense, since trial witnesses had stated that Liddy had gotten all that money from CRP specifically to pay for the burglary and whatever other expenses might be involved. Liddy was just as much a part of the burglary as if he had been caught inside DNC Campaign Headquarters as James McCord had been.

In late afternoon on January 30, the case went to the jury.

The Verdict and Its Consequences

Ninety minutes after receiving the case, the jury returned with its verdicts:

G. Gordon Liddy: guilty on five separate counts of conspiracy, burglary, illegal wiretapping.

James W. McCord Jr.: guilty on eight separate counts of conspiracy, burglary, illegal wiretapping.

Two days later Judge John Sirica set bail for each defendant at one hundred thousand dollars. He deferred sentencing until the last week in March, and he indicated he would also sentence the five Miami men who had pled guilty at the same time.

Then, the judge had one more thing to say: "I am still not satisfied that all the pertinent facts that might be available—I say might be available—have been produced before an American jury."[1] He seemed to be saying: There's got to be more, this is not the complete story.

The Democrats, feeling humiliated by their overwhelming election defeat the previous November, looked to rebalance the scales. Rumors of Republican dirty tricks had been swirling around, and the notion that there could be more severe campaign violations lay just under the surface. There were, also, those *Washington Post* revelations from Bob Woodward and Carl Bernstein about hush money and the ties between the burglary, the White House, and the Committee to Re-elect the President. There were even suspicions that a cover-up seeking to protect high-level Republicans had been conducted.

The Senate Watergate Committee

The Democrats in Congress struck in early February. They persuaded Republicans to join them, and the Senate created a Select Committee on Presidential Campaign Activities. It would be four Democrats and three Republicans under the chairmanship of Democratic Senator Sam Ervin of North Carolina, a rumpled, courtly southerner with a Harvard law–trained mind.

The vote to create the committee was 77–0.

At the same time, the Senate Judiciary Committee was ready to consider the nomination of L. Patrick Gray to be permanent FBI director. It was the committee's duty to recommend confirmation to the full Senate of certain high-level candidates for government jobs. Gray, who had limited the initial FBI investigation into the break-in, who had allowed White House lawyers to sit in while his agents interviewed CRP employees, and who had passed FBI interview reports to John Dean to prepare witnesses for FBI interviews, had done what the White House asked him to do, and now he expected his reward: to be named permanent FBI director.

Judge Sirica said: "I am still not satisfied that all the pertinent facts that might be available . . . have been produced before an American jury."

But within hours, L. Patrick Gray created a major problem. He testified that John Dean had seen whatever the FBI uncovered in the Watergate investigation, and that Gray, himself, had often discussed the investigation's progress with the White House.[2]

Then John Dean should come here and testify, one of the senators demanded.

Nixon would not allow it. "No President could ever agree to allow the counsel to the President to go down and testify before a committee," he stated.[3] Nixon was invoking executive privilege, under which he could prevent his private presidential conversations from being aired.

As the Senate Judiciary Committee hearings continued, Gray offered the written interviews his agents had collected. One was with Herbert Kalmbach, Nixon's

Executive Privilege

The idea of executive privilege and whether a president can claim it to withhold information from Congress dates to the days of George Washington. It is based on protecting a president's right to receive confidential information from his closest advisers without fear that such information could be disclosed. Its supported by "separation of powers" under which no branch of U.S. government can compel another branch to disclose information because all have equal and separate power. While the Constitution does not mention executive privilege, U.S. presidents have argued that it is implied because the executive branch has power equal to and separate from that of Congress and the judiciary.

This was the argument Richard Nixon used to withhold tapes from Special Prosecutor Leon Jaworski. But the U.S. Supreme Court ruled unanimously that executive privilege is not absolute; it does not apply when crimes are involved (such as obstruction of justice, perjury, or conspiracy). So the Court required Nixon to give up the tapes.

Presidents continue to assert executive privilege. Both Bill Clinton and George W. Bush have claimed it, withholding information on grounds of national security and of preserving confidentiality with key advisers. Congress, on the other hand, continues to believe it has the right to such information.

West Coast fund-raiser and lawyer. It spelled out the dirty tricks of Donald Segretti in the 1972 presidential campaign. In his FBI interview, Kalmbach stated that he had been contacted by Dwight Chapin, Nixon's appointments secretary, and told to get in touch with Segretti. According to Kalmbach, Chapin said that Segretti "may be of service to the Republican Party."[4] He admitted he had paid Segretti to perform the dirty tricks.

It was now clear: The Chapin connection meant that the White House had authorized the dirty tricks.

A Cancer on the Presidency

A few weeks later, on March 21, John Dean walked into Nixon's office. What the two talked about was not made public for more than a year, but their words came back to haunt them both. Dean believed the spreading illegal activities were "a cancer on the Presidency" that needed to be removed. He mentioned that the cover-up and the payment of the hush money involved not only himself, but Bob Haldeman, John Ehrlichman, and John Mitchell. In a conspiratorial tone, Nixon seemed to acknowledge Dean's words: "You're taking care of the witnesses," he affirmed.[5]

Then, to the hush money:

"How much money do you need?" the president asked.

"I would say these people are going to cost a million dollars. . . . " Dean answered.

"We could get that," Nixon stated.[6]

They moved to L. Patrick Gray's damaging testimony, especially about Dean himself.

Former White House counsel John Dean testifies before the Senate Watergate committee in June 1973. Dean had told Nixon that the illegal campaign activities constituted "a cancer on the presidency."

"Your cover's broken," Nixon told him. "Let's suppose that you and Haldeman and Ehrlichman and Mitchell say, 'We can't hold this.' What, what, then, are you going to say?"[7]

Neither had an answer for that. They turned to a discussion of E. Howard Hunt and whether he could be granted executive clemency for his crimes. Nixon stated he could not grant clemency for at least a year and a half, if then.

"That's right," Dean agreed. "It may further involve you in a way you shouldn't be involved in this."

Then, a little later, Nixon sighed. "We're all in on it."[8]

That conversation, however, was still unknown to the general public, which was awaiting the sentencing of the Watergate burglary defendants. What the public and the defendants did not know was that Judge Sirica had received James McCord's bombshell letter, alleging political pressure for the defendants to plead guilty and keep their mouths shut and saying that "perjury occurred during the trial" and that "others involved in the Watergate operation were not identified."

Two days after the Nixon-Dean meeting, Judge Sirica looked over the large crowd of spectators in his courtroom and announced: "There is a preliminary matter to take up before I impose sentences. . . . "[9]

He read James McCord's letter to the stunned courtroom.

After a short recess, Sirica began to pass sentences on the defendants: for G. Gordon Liddy, who had been defiant throughout the trial, often clowning and waving to the spectators and the jury, twenty years and a fine of forty thousand dollars, with no chance for parole until he had served six years and eight months. For Bernard Barker, Eugenio Martínez, Frank Sturgis, and Virgilio González, forty years. For E. Howard Hunt, thirty-five years. All the sentences except for Liddy's were provisional, meaning that the judge would watch how they cooperated with the Senate Committee (now called the "Ervin Committee" after its chairman) investigating campaign activities during the 1972 presidential election, which included the primaries as well as Watergate. If they cooperated, the sentences could be reduced.

The Cover-up Unravels

It was not long before the Ervin Committee contacted McCord. Yes, he would testify about what he knew, but he wanted to do so in front of the senators and under oath. Senator Ervin agreed but insisted it would be a closed session of the committee, no public, no reporters; just McCord, his lawyer, the senators, and their staffs.

That was fine with McCord, and by the end of March 1973, he had named names for the senators: John Mitchell, Charles Colson, John Dean, Jeb Magruder—all had knowledge of the Watergate operation. Even though this testimony was supposed to be secret, some leaked out, and the *Los Angeles Times* reported that, according to McCord, both Dean and Magruder had known of the Watergate burglary in advance.[10] But McCord went even further; he testified that Liddy told him the break-in and the wiretapping had been approved by John Mitchell while Mitchell was attorney general of the United States.

As this information began to appear in newspapers and on radio and television, the cover-up slowly fell apart. First to crack was John Dean, who had started talking to the prosecutors in the first week of April because he sensed he was being set up by the Nixon administration to take full blame for the cover-up. A few days earlier, in late March, the prosecutors had reconvened the Watergate grand jury, and Judge Sirica had gone along with their request to grant immunity from further prosecution to the seven Watergate defendants (now all convicted) if they told their complete stories to the grand jury.

Jeb Magruder could sense the ground falling away from under him. His name had surfaced in James McCord's testimony. John Dean had refused to promise Magruder that he would maintain the cover story they had agreed to the previous summer about not being a part of Gemstone and not meeting with Liddy about it.[11] Then the *Washington Post* reported that the Ervin Committee wanted to talk with Magruder's assistant, and Magruder knew the assistant could tie him in to the planning for Gemstone.[12]

After a week of nervous hand-wringing, Magruder finally decided to talk to the prosecutors. He described his role in the Watergate break-in, the cover-up, and the payment of hush money. He admitted that he had committed perjury numerous times, including his testimony at the Watergate break-in trial when he denied knowing what G. Gordon Liddy had planned with Gemstone.

Richard Nixon's White House was coming apart. James McCord, John Dean, and Jeb Magruder were talking to the prosecutors, and they were implicating

Bob Haldeman and John Ehrlichman, the two men closest to Richard Nixon.

As John Dean, in his grand jury testimony, implicated more of the people around Richard Nixon in the break-in, the cover-up, the payment of hush money, even promises of executive clemency, the atmosphere at the White House grew more anxious. Dean became the butt of nasty comments: He's "an unbelievable disaster for us," said Haldeman; a "piranha," said Ehrlichman; "an evil man," said Nixon.[13] But all recognized the danger: Cutting Dean loose would allow him to blame Haldeman, Ehrlichman, and the president for many of the Watergate disasters. Only if Haldeman and Ehrlichman went too could Nixon ride things out.

On April 30, 1973, with Nixon's encouragement, Haldeman and Ehrlichman reluctantly resigned, and John Dean was fired. Then, Nixon turned to his attorney general, Richard Kleindienst, who was friendly with potential Watergate defendants. What he needed, Nixon decided, was a new team in place, one not tainted by any smudge from Watergate.[14] So he asked for Kleindienst's resignation, too. And earlier, he had made it clear that L. Patrick Gray no longer had his support for FBI director.

On May 1, 1973, Alexander Haig, a four-star general and a strong Nixon ally, agreed to become the new chief of staff at the White House; Elliot Richardson, the secretary of defense, had agreed to become the new attorney general; and William Ruckelshaus, director of the Environmental Protection Agency, had agreed to become FBI director. In announcing these changes

Nixon pledged, "I will do everything in my power to ensure that the guilty are brought to justice."[15]

If Nixon counted on his new team to turn public opinion around, he was to be sadly mistaken. Within days, the Gallup polling organization asked Americans whether they thought Nixon had been personally involved in the Watergate cover-up: Fifty percent, one out of two, said yes, he had been involved.[16]

The Hearings Begin

About two weeks later, on May 17, 1973, the Ervin Committee hearings opened in room 318 in the Old Senate Office Building, an ornate room with mighty pillars, mahogany paneling, and chandeliers. The seven members of the committee, backed by their staffs, sat with Senator Sam Ervin presiding. Facing them was a table with several chairs and a desk microphone. Most witnesses, after being sworn in, read an opening statement to the committee. Each member of the committee would then question the witness. Ervin, with his courtly manner, set the tone for the hearings: mutual respect, polite behavior, carefully phrased questions and responses. By the time these hearings concluded four months later, thirty-three witnesses had appeared, 237 hours of testimony had been televised, and almost nine out of ten Americans had watched at least a portion of the hearings.[17]

On the second day of hearings, James McCord reviewed the way he and the Plumbers had committed the burglary. He stated that both Liddy and Hunt had told him that John Mitchell, John Dean, and Jeb Magruder had approved the overall operation. He said he had been promised financial support if he remained silent and that he could expect executive clemency somewhere down the line.[18]

Executive clemency—only the president could make that happen! Nixon was now implicated in the Watergate affair. It was no longer just a possibility or a theory.

Then, the latest threat to Nixon took shape. The Senate decided that a special prosecutor with subpoena powers should be appointed to look into all the Watergate matters because things were becoming so complicated. The appointment would be approved by the Senate, with the Department of Justice choosing the person who could only be dismissed by the attorney general for "extraordinary improprieties."

In short order, Attorney General Elliot Richardson had appointed Harvard law professor Archibald Cox as special prosecutor, and the Senate quickly confirmed him. Cox had been solicitor general in the administration of the late John F. Kennedy—the same Kennedy who had defeated Richard Nixon in 1960 for the presidency.

At the other end of Pennsylvania Avenue, Sam Ervin slowly built the case against Richard Nixon, starting with the actual burglars, then working up the line to the people who made the big decisions. As the weeks went by, Hugh Sloan testified that John Mitchell had authorized the money Liddy received from CRP. Maurice Stans, CRP's former treasurer, testified to pretty much the same thing. A bit later came Jeb Magruder, now sorry for his involvement in the burglary and the cover-up, but clear about who, besides himself, was involved: John Mitchell . . . Charles Colson . . . John Dean.

Then John Dean testified. Rumors and theories about how much he knew had swirled about Capitol Hill. But two things were acknowledged: Dean had been talking with the prosecutors and the grand jury for two months, and he had been deeply implicated by others in the Watergate break-in and cover-up.

On June 25, 1973, Dean settled himself alone at the table in front of the senators. "The Watergate matter," he said quietly, "was an inevitable outgrowth of a climate of excessive concern over the political impact of demonstrators, excessive concern over leaks, an insatiable appetite for political intelligence, all coupled with a do-it-yourself White House staff, regardless of the law."[19]

In those few words, John Dean had nailed the situation: The White House was so upset about leaks and political demonstrations, so eager to learn what their opponents were thinking and planning, that staying within the law was not a consideration.

He offered facts, dates, conversations, and analysis in an unhurried, flat voice, as if he were reading a report to a group of businessmen. He mentioned Richard Nixon, Bob Haldeman, and John Ehrlichman in establishing the wide-ranging White House conspiracy to cover up who was involved in the Watergate burglary, why the burglary was committed, who paid for it, where the money came from, and what they had hoped to accomplish.

When he was finished, Dean had accused Nixon of criminal acts, mainly obstruction of justice, and it was a stunning event. It would become Richard Nixon's word against John Dean's word, and the committee wondered whether they should call Nixon to testify.

The Oval Office Tapes

Nixon moved quickly. A few days after Dean's testimony, he sent a letter to Ervin: "I shall not testify before the Committee," he wrote, "or permit access to Presidential papers." In essence, Nixon was declaring: One branch of the government cannot force another branch to do anything, we are coequal, I have as much power as you do.[20]

There matters stood, each side glaring at the other, refusing to back down—and then Alexander Butterfield testified. Butterfield had been a deputy assistant to the president and a close aide of Bob Haldeman. One of his responsibilities had been internal security at the White House, and no one expected anything dramatic. But committee lawyers did wonder about documents that had come to them from the White House, which described conversations between John Dean and Nixon in detail. How were they able to get so much? Who took it all down?

After some fencing, it finally came out. "Mr. Butterfield," one of the committee lawyers asked, "are you aware of any listening devices in the Oval Office of the President?"

"I was aware of listening devices, yes sir," Butterfield admitted.[21]

The hearing room sat in stunned silence. The president had been taping his conversations, and he had been doing it for years.

The tape recorder used in the Nixon White House to record conversations in the Oval Office. The existence of a secret recording system blew the Watergate case wide open.

It meant the president's words could now be checked, and John Dean's charges could now be tested.

Nixon put up a stiff front: "Let others wallow in Watergate," he stated a week later. He intended to move on; the past was the past. The committee asked him for copies of all documents and tapes that related to Watergate. The president refused on the grounds of executive privilege, saying that as president, he was a coequal branch of government, and Congress could not force him to give up anything he did not want to give up. In any case, he wrote, the tapes were "entirely consistent with what I know to be the truth."[22]

The senators wanted more than Nixon's word alone. They issued a subpoena for several conversations between Nixon and John Dean, which then made the tapes potential evidence. If anyone destroyed them, it would be a crime: obstruction of justice.

The same day, Special Prosecutor Archibald Cox issued *his* subpoena for nine additional tapes, all of them Nixon conversations with Haldeman, Ehrlichman, John Mitchell, and/or John Dean on specific dates. Both subpoenas were hand-delivered to the White House on July 23, 1973.

Three days later Richard Nixon rejected the subpoenas, and the battle went on.

It was Watergate Judge John Sirica's turn to rule on the question of the president's right to withhold information because of "executive privilege," since the Watergate grand jury also wanted the information.

Nixon's lawyer argued the president was "beyond the process of any court," he and the courts were coequal branches of the government (just as the president and

Congress were coequal branches), and one branch cannot force another branch to divulge private conversations because they were "privileged"—and a subpoena is an attempt to "force" the president to do this.[23]

Cox countered that executive privilege did not apply when there was "strong reason to believe that the integrity of the executive office had been corrupted."[24] In other words, if a crime has been committed, there is no executive privilege.

Sirica agreed with Cox, saying just because it was the president who held the evidence (the tapes) was no reason to stop the court from getting it.

But Richard Nixon was not finished. He appealed Sirica's decision to the court of appeals, and for the moment, he could hang on to his tapes.

The Saturday Night Massacre

In the meantime, Nixon was not happy with Archibald Cox, the special prosecutor. Cox's connections with the Kennedys and his patrician personality made him highly suspicious to Nixon, who had grown up in a relatively poor, unsophisticated family.

It did not help that Cox was able to get guilty pleas from some of the higher-ups in the Watergate affair. His strategy was simple: If they pled guilty and agreed to testify against others, they could receive less severe sentences. On August 16, Jeb Magruder pled guilty to perjury and obstruction of justice; on September 17, Donald Segretti pled guilty to multiple campaign violations; then, on October 19, the biggest catch of all: John Dean pled guilty to conspiracy to obstruct justice.

A week before the Dean guilty plea, the court of appeals decided the presidential tapes case: By a 5–2 vote they decided Nixon must give up the tapes requested by the special prosecutor. But Nixon considered appealing to the U.S. Supreme Court, where a final decision would not come for months. He would not have to share his tapes—at least for a while.

He had another alternative, too. On the evening of October 19—the same day John Dean pled guilty in criminal court—Nixon issued a public statement that he was directing Cox to issue no more subpoenas "to obtain tapes, notes or memoranda of Presidential conversations."[25]

Cox, however, refused to comply. Would he resign? "No!" he stated to a reporter. "No!"[26]

The next day, Nixon instructed Attorney General Elliot Richardson to fire Cox. Richardson, who had given assurances to the Senate that the special prosecutor's independence would be scrupulously observed, no matter what, refused.

Then he resigned as attorney general.

In a few moments, the president's order was relayed to FBI Director William Ruckelshaus, the second-in-command at the Department of Justice: Fire Archibald Cox.

Ruckelshaus refused and was fired.

The same order was then given to Solicitor General Robert Bork, third-in-command at the Department of Justice. Robert Bork did as he was told and carried out the firing. Archibald Cox was no longer the special prosecutor.

Participants and victims in the "Saturday Night Massacre": Watergate Special Prosecutor Archibald Cox refused to resign at Nixon's request. Attorney General Elliot Richardson refused to fire him and resigned. Attorney General William Ruckelshaus refused to fire Cox and was fired. Finally, Solicitor General Robert Bork agreed to fire Cox.

Within twenty-four hours, the series of firings and resignations had a name: "Saturday Night Massacre." The American people reacted angrily; many thousands of telegrams poured into the White House condemning Nixon's actions. Newspapers across the country blasted the president for what they considered unprincipled actions. Even Judge Sirica got in the act; he considered fining the White House thousands of dollars per day because Nixon so far had refused to give up the tapes in spite of the judge's order.[27]

Several days later, motions for the impeachment of Richard Nixon had been filed in the House of Representatives, including one by a Republican, Pete McCloskey of California. It would be the first impeachment in over one hundred years, with the possibility of a trial and removal of a sitting president for "high crimes and misdemeanors," as the U.S. Constitution requires. The impeachment motions were referred to the House Judiciary Committee, whose chairman, Peter Rodino, stated on October 23, 1973, that "formal preparations" had begun.[28]

That same day, Nixon's lawyers advised Sirica that they would make the subpoenaed tapes available to the special prosecutor's office.

"The court is very happy," Judge Sirica informed them.[29]

A New Special Prosecutor

Shortly thereafter, a new special prosecutor was appointed: Leon Jaworski, an eminent Texas lawyer who had supported Nixon for reelection. But if Nixon sought comfort from this, he would be sadly rebuffed.

Jaworski received seven tapes from the judge, listened to them, and quietly advised Alexander Haig, Nixon's chief of staff, that the president ought to consider hiring a criminal lawyer. Jaworski heard Nixon and Dean speak of paying hush money, of knowing about the cover-up from shortly after the burglary at the Watergate, and of destroying documents and files that might be incriminating.[30] The tapes proved that John Dean's testimony before the Ervin Committee about the White House role in the burglary and the cover-up had been the truth.

But there was more. In reviewing one tape, Leon Jaworski heard the president advise Bob Haldeman about how to testify under oath and avoid incriminating himself when asked about hush money payoffs.

"Just be damned sure you say 'I don't remember; I can't recall; I can't give any honest, an answer to that that I can recall. . . . '" Jaworski heard Nixon say.

The special prosecutor's face got red. "Can you imagine that?" he said. "The President of the United States sitting in his office telling his staff how to commit perjury!"[31]

There were other problems with the tapes. Nine had been subpoenaed, but only seven had been located, and the White House had no explanation why two were missing.

The conversations must not have been recorded, the White House offered. Maybe the tape ran out before the conversations happened?[32]

"ENOUGH IS ENOUGH," declared the *Detroit Free Press.*

"A TRAGIC POINT OF NO RETURN," stated *Time Magazine*.[33]

Then, a couple of days later, another finding: A tape of the first Watergate conversation Nixon had with Haldeman after the burglary showed a buzzing that blotted out conversation for eighteen and one-half minutes. They played the tape in open court before Judge Sirica, and the buzzing was there for all to hear. But no one ever admitted responsibility.

Unindicted Coconspirator

In the meantime, the Watergate grand jury had been hearing testimony about the payment of hush money, the cover-up, and acts of obstruction of justice as well as perjury. As the tapes became available, and Richard Nixon's own words showed how deeply he had been involved, the prosecutors wanted to establish his role in some formal way. They could not indict him (the Constitution limits the actions that can be taken against a sitting president), but, somehow, they wanted to tie him in.

On February 25, 1974, they found a way. The grand jury voted unanimously, with one abstention, to list Richard Nixon as an *unindicted coconspirator* "to defraud the United States and to obstruct justice."[34]

By this time, Jeb Magruder, Donald Segretti, Herbert Kalmbach, and John Dean had already pled guilty, and on March 1, 1974, the grand jury indicted John Mitchell, Bob Haldeman, John Ehrlichman, Charles Colson, and several others with conspiracy to obstruct justice and with a series of other crimes, including perjury.[35]

Nixon would not stand with them, but his shadow would be over them. In an ominous step, the grand jury packaged up the evidence and turned copies over to the House Judiciary Committee, which was considering whether to impeach Nixon. In early April, the House Judiciary Committee issued a subpoena for forty-six tapes and warned that if Nixon did not give them up, his refusal might be considered "contempt of Congress."[36]

Nixon, however, continued to bob and weave. He went on television to say he would make available his "edited" version of the tapes, and alongside him viewers could see a large pile of bound transcripts, some twelve hundred pages worth. *I'm telling the truth!* he seemed to be saying.[37]

At the same time, Special Prosecutor Jaworski issued a subpoena for sixty-four more Nixon tapes, and to Jaworski as well as the House Judiciary Committee, Nixon said simply, No! No more tapes. "He is up for the battle," said his spokesperson, "he intends to fight it, and he feels he has a personal and a constitutional duty to do so."[38]

Then, an event three thousand miles away brought a new challenge. Months before, a Los Angeles grand jury had indicted several people close to the president in the burglary of the office of Daniel Ellsberg's psychiatrist, Lewis Fielding. One of them was Colson, Nixon's special assistant; now, with the tape controversy and the serious impeachment inquiry going forward in Washington, word had just come in: Colson had agreed to plead guilty to obstructing justice in the Ellsberg/Fielding burglary case and agreed to testify against the other defendants. Jaworski, in the meantime, decided to go

President Nixon poses with transcripts of the White House tapes, which he proposed to turn over to the House Judiciary Committee instead of the tapes themselves.

right to the U.S. Supreme Court for a final decision on the Nixon tapes, and the Court agreed to hear the case in early July 1974.

Impeachment

At the House Judiciary Committee, a staff of forty lawyers were sifting through the impeachment evidence. The committee had the records of the Ervin Watergate Committee; it had the secret Watergate grand jury testimony; it had notes and conclusions from the special prosecutor's investigation; it even had the tapes the special prosecutor had forced the White House to give up.

For impeachment, a majority of the thirty-eight person Judiciary Committee had to be in favor. There were twenty-one Democrats and seventeen Republicans on the committee, so Richard Nixon needed to convince two Democrats he had done nothing wrong, while keeping all the Republicans on his side. That would make a tie vote, and the impeachment would fail.

The committee was not happy with the "edited" versions of the tapes Nixon had supplied, and Chairman Peter Rodino sent a letter to the White House stating he had failed to comply with the subpoena for the tapes. First, a single Republican committee member, then two more Republican members, joined the Democrats in supporting the letter, and suddenly Richard Nixon was facing bipartisan disapproval.[39]

On July 19, 1974, the committee, through its chief lawyer, issued a 306-page "Summary of Information" from six weeks of closed-door hearings and examination of documents and tapes—and twenty-nine proposed articles of impeachment against Richard Nixon!

For the first time, the public could see, in specific terms, how Richard Nixon would be charged. The committee's lawyer, in presenting the accusations, put it starkly: "Reasonable men acting reasonably would find the President guilty."[40]

Over the next few days, Republicans and Democrats met to go over the charges, and gradually they narrowed them to two main points: abuse of power and obstruction

The Impeachment of President Andrew Johnson

The first American president to be impeached was Andrew Johnson, who had been Abraham Lincoln's vice president and assumed the presidency following Lincoln's assassination in 1865. Three years later, in the midst of Reconstruction and lingering animosities from the Civil War, Johnson attempted to fire Secretary of War Edwin Stanton. Stanton refused to leave, claiming that only Congress could remove him under the recently passed Tenure of Office Act (which Congress had passed over Johnson's veto). Congress considered Johnson's firing of Stanton a violation of the Tenure of Office Act, and eleven articles of impeachment were drawn up. A trial—in accordance with the Constitution—was held in the Senate, and on May 16, 1868, by a margin of one vote, Andrew Johnson was acquitted.

In the summer of 1974, more than one hundred years later, Richard Nixon became the next American president to face charges of impeachment, though he resigned before there could be a trial in the Senate.

of justice. Still, most Republicans on the committee continued to support Nixon.

But all of that changed on July 24, 1974, when the U.S. Supreme Court decided whether Nixon could use executive privilege to withhold tapes from the special prosecutor. By a vote of 8–0, the Court said no. The president could not place himself above the law, the Court stated. He could not claim a right to keep something confidential and compromise the fairness of an impending criminal trial. Nixon would have to give up the actual tapes.

It was a body blow to Nixon's defense. Within hours, Richard Nixon gave a public statement: "I respect and accept the court's decision," he said with obvious disappointment.[41]

Simultaneously, the House Judiciary Committee held public debate on whether to impeach the president.

"I am not going to sit here and be an idle spectator to the diminution, the subversion, the destruction of the Constitution," said Texas Democrat Barbara Jordan.[42]

But, said Michigan Republican Edward Hutchinson, "the Committee has not resolved just what an impeachable offense is."[43]

On the evening of July 27, 1974, the committee voted on the first article of impeachment: obstruction of justice. Twenty-seven voted aye; eleven voted no. Six Republicans had joined the Democrats.

Two days later, the committee voted on the second article of impeachment: abuse of power. Twenty-eight voted aye; ten voted no. Seven Republicans had joined the Democrats.

Faced with a vote to impeach in the House of Representatives, Nixon resigned the presidency. Here he boards a helicopter and bids goodbye to his staff with his well-known "victory" salute.

The next day, July 30, 1974, the committee voted on the third article of impeachment: contempt of Congress. Twenty-one voted aye; seventeen voted no. Three Republicans had joined the Democrats.

For the first time in 106 years, a president of the United States was on the verge of impeachment. What lay ahead was a trial on the impeachment charges before the chief justice of the United States, with the entire U.S. Senate as the jury.

What would Richard Nixon do? On August 2, 1974, came a reminder of how Watergate had altered some people's lives: Judge Sirica sentenced John Dean to a minimum of one year in prison.

A Lewis Harris poll showed that more than two out of three Americans favored Richard Nixon's impeachment.[44]

Nixon's cabinet, some Republican members of both the Senate and House of Representatives, even his personal advisers urged him to resign. A delegation of the Republican leadership in Congress—Senator Barry Goldwater, Senator Hugh Scott, and Congressman John Rhodes—came to the White House and told him he could count on no more than fifteen senators (less than half he needed) to vote against his impeachment.

Finally, on the evening of Thursday, August 8, 1974, Nixon went on television and resigned as president of the United States, effective at noon the next day. "I have never been a quitter," he stated, but "I must put the interests of America first."[45]

Six years earlier, on the same month and the same day, he had accepted the Republican nomination for the presidency. Now it was over.

The Movie: All the President's Men

This film covers seven months from the early morning hours of June 17, 1972, to the presidential inauguration of Richard Nixon on January 20, 1973, mostly seen through the eyes of *Washington Post* reporters Carl Bernstein and Bob Woodward. It opens in January 1973, with Richard Nixon arriving with a police escort at the U.S. Capitol in Washington to give his State of the Union address to Congress, following his reelection to the presidency in November. Nixon strides into the Senate chamber, greeting people on both sides, "a happy president," says the narrator as Nixon mounts the dais and prepares to speak.

88

▮▯▮▯▮▯▮▯▮▯▮▯▮▯▮▯▮▯▮▯▮▯▮▯▮▯▮▯▮▯▮

Then, the scene changes and goes back to the early morning of June 17, 1972, where five men are burglarizing the offices of the Democratic National Committee in Washington's Watergate complex. The police suddenly arrive, confront the burglars, and arrest them. The police soon discover links between the burglars and the White House and pass the information on to Bernstein and Woodward. The reporters find out about "dirty tricks" by Republicans against Democratic candidates during the ongoing 1972 presidential campaign. They also discover that large amounts of money—"campaign contributions"—are flowing into Republican hands for use in the campaign. Woodward meets "Deep Throat," a secret U.S. government source, who tells him to "follow the money." He and Bernstein discover funds in a burglar's bank account that came from political contributions to the committee that will run Nixon's reelection campaign (the Committee to Re-elect the President, or CRP). Much of the CRP money is cash, and a CRP bookkeeper tells them there is a political slush fund at CRP controlled by top Republicans that contains hundreds of thousands of dollars. Woodward and Bernstein figure that this paid for the Watergate burglary, and the *Washington Post* runs their "slush fund" story.

They tie "dirty tricks" to the White House and find a cover-up because the FBI was prevented from investigating the connection between the burglary and Nixon's advisers. John Mitchell, one-time attorney general and director of CRP, knew about the burglary, Deep Throat says.

The reporters discover that five people control the slush fund, and they decide that one has to be Bob

A scene from the movie *All the President's Men* shows the burglary of Democratic National Committee headquarters at the Watergate.

Haldeman, Nixon's chief of staff. Because they misunderstand one of their sources, they publish a story stating that Haldeman had been named to the grand jury when that was not the case. Much criticism from the Nixon people ensues.

Deep Throat tells Woodward that the story is correct, "it was a Haldeman operation all the way." The entire U.S. intelligence operation is involved, Deep Throat adds, "it leads everywhere." He also warns Woodward that his and Bernstein's lives are in danger.

The reporters wake Ben Bradlee, executive editor of the *Washington Post*, to tell him they can confirm what they have reported, and there is a massive cover-up going on over the burglary, the slush fund, and the dirty tricks. Bradlee responds: "Nothing's riding on this except the First Amendment of the Constitution, freedom of the press and maybe the future of this country."

The final movie scene is the *Washington Post* newsroom on January 20, 1973, with television screens showing Richard Nixon taking the presidential oath of office, following his reelection. In the background are chattering teletypes, and in close-up the machines print what will happen during the next nineteen months: guilty pleas and convictions of each person involved in the burglary, the dirty tricks, the slush fund, and the cover-up.

And finally, the resignation of Richard Nixon.

Inside the Movie

While the basic filming location was in and around the Watergate complex at 2600 Virginia Avenue NW, Washington, D.C., some scenes were shot elsewhere. For example, the early-morning scene in the parking garage where Bob Woodward meets Deep Throat, presumed to be somewhere in Washington, was actually filmed at the ABC Entertainment Center in Century City, California. The scene in Donald Segretti's apartment (location never identified) with Carl Bernstein where they discuss the "dirty tricks" campaign was shot at Marina del Rey, an upscale residential

The cast of *All the President's Men* contained many fine actors and actresses. Here are some of them, their roles in the movie, and other movies they were in and awards they have won.

Bob Woodward (reporter)—Robert Redford: two Academy Award nominations, one Oscar: *Ordinary People* (1980) for Best Director.

Carl Bernstein (reporter)—Dustin Hoffman: seven Academy award nominations, two Oscars: *Kramer vs. Kramer* (1979) and *Rain Main* (1988).

Harry M. Rosenfeld (Metro News Editor, *Washington Post*)— Jack Warden (d. 2006): two Academy Award nominations.

Howard Simons (Managing Editor, *Washington Post*)—Martin Balsam (d. 1996): one Oscar: *A Thousand Clowns* (1965).

Deep Throat (Woodward source)—Hal Holbrook: one Academy Award nomination.

Ben Bradlee (Executive Editor, *Washington Post*)—Jason Robards: two Oscars: *All the President's Men* (1976), *Julia* (1977).

Judy Hoback (CRP accountant)—Jane Alexander: four Academy Award nominations.

Debbie Sloan (Hugh Sloan's wife)—Meredith Baxter: three Emmy nominations.

Martin Dardis (Florida DA)—Ned Beatty: one Academy Award nomination.

Hugh Sloan (Assistant Treasurer, CRP)—Stephen Collins: one Emmy nomination; published three novels; starred in *Star Trek: The Motion Picture* (1978) and the TV series *Seventh Heaven*.

Sgt. Paul Leeper (an arresting officer at Watergate Hotel)— F. Murray Abraham: one Oscar: *Amadeus* (1984).

Robert Redford as Bob Woodward and Dustin Hoffman as Carl Bernstein collaborate on a Watergate story for the *Washington Post*.

community on the water in Los Angeles. The scene where Carl Bernstein goes to the Justice Building in Dade County, Florida, to meet with District Attorney Martin Dardis was actually filmed in downtown Los Angeles.

Even with a carefully put together movie like this, several filming "goofs" did occur:

- When Woodward and Bernstein go to see Judy Hoback, the bookkeeper, the level of tea in the tea pitcher changes from a front shot to a back shot, and a newspaper appears and disappears between camera shots.

- When Ben Bradlee shouts "Woodstein!" after getting a phone call from the White House, there is a boom mike visible at the bottom left of the screen.

- When Woodward and Bernstein go to Hugh Sloan's home and talk in his living room, the cushions on the sofa change between shots.

- Overhead shots of Bob Woodward driving out of the parking complex at two different times, weeks apart, show the same people moving about on the sidewalk.

And there are these little-known facts:

- *All the President's Men* was the first film Jimmy Carter viewed in the White House when he became president in 1977.

- Originally, British film director John Schlesinger was offered the director's job, but he turned it down. He felt it should be directed by an American. Alan J. Pakula, the ultimate director, was born in the Bronx, New York, and spent his career in Hollywood.

- During the entire filming in Washington, D.C., star Robert Redford stayed at the actual Watergate Hotel.

- The Miami scene in which Carl Bernstein outsmarts security to see District Attorney Martin Dardis never actually happened. It is pure fiction.

- When Bob Woodward dials the White House to get confirmation on a story, he uses the then-actual White House phone number: 456–1414.

Special Touches

Drama, mystery, and suspense played big roles in the film. Movie ads blared: "The most devastating detective story of the century!" and "At times it looked like it might cost them their jobs, their reputations, and maybe even their lives." Old-fashioned cloak-and-dagger portrayals popped up again and again:

- the spooky late-night meetings between Woodward and Deep Throat in the empty parking garage
- the secret-code newspaper and flower pot messages Woodward and Deep Throat leave one another
- the ruses Carl Bernstein uses to see District Attorney Martin Dardis in Miami
- the warning Deep Throat gives Woodward and Bernstein that their lives could be in danger

Suspense certainly added to the mystery and drama. Would Woodward and Bernstein be able to track down those who made the illegal campaign contributions? Who was behind the Watergate burglary in the first place, and why was it done? Where would all this lead? As the reporters follow the trail step-by-step, they find themselves struggling to convince their bosses at the *Washington Post* that they are uncovering a major political conspiracy.

In the movie, editor Ben Bradlee says, "Nothing's riding on this except the First Amendment of the Constitution, freedom of the press and maybe the future of this country."

Among the famous actors in the movie were (from left) Dustin Hoffman, Robert Redford, Jason Robards, Jack Warden, and Martin Balsam. Robards received an Academy Award for his portrayal of *Washington Post* executive editor Ben Bradlee.

With each step they take, from getting a list of major contributors to CRP to interviewing employees of CRP to getting confirmation on those who controlled the slush fund, there is a gradual buildup of the political conspiracy case. But they face constant obstacles: People hang up on them, do not return their phone calls, and complain about them to their bosses.

Yet, they get more and more of the story.

How they get it is shown by the way they interview. Patience and perseverance play out in Carl Bernstein's excruciating long interview with bookkeeper Judy Hoback where he drinks cup after cup of coffee and finally gets confirmation of the existence of the slush fund. Warmth and concern play out as Woodward and Bernstein visit Hugh Sloan, whose wife is in the hospital, and by asking gentle, almost apologetic questions, gain the names of those running the slush fund. Innocent uncertainty plays out as Bob Woodward seeks confirmation on political contributions from those at CRP and the White House.

Suspense finally comes to a head when Woodward meets Deep Throat in the empty garage and Deep Throat tells him there is a wide political conspiracy that "leads everywhere."

Behind the Camera

The producer of *All the President's Men* was Walter Coblenz, who has produced a total of seventeen major feature films in his career. This was his fourth and by far his most successful. Robert Redford was also a producer. The director was Alan J. Pakula (d. 1998) who directed sixteen films (and produced eighteen) during his career. He was nominated for three Oscars, including a nomination for *All the President's Men*. Two of his Oscar nominations were for directing and one (*Sophie's Choice*, 1982) was for screenwriting. William Goldman, a successful novelist and Broadway playwright, wrote the screenplay and won an Oscar for his work on *All the President's Men*. He has written more than twenty-five screenplays, and one of them, *Butch Cassidy and the Sundance Kid*, received the Oscar in 1970 for screenwriting.

Popular Response

The movie was released in 1976 and became the second biggest film of the year (after *One Flew Over the Cuckoo's Nest*). It received eight Academy Award nominations and won four Academy Awards: Jason Robards for Best Supporting Actor, playing *Washington Post* executive editor Ben Bradlee, Best Screenplay Adaptation (from Bob Woodward and Carl Bernstein's 1974 book, *All the President's Men*); Best Art Direction; and Best Sound. It was also nominated for Best Picture, though it lost out to *Rocky*. Reviews of the movie were uniformly good, using words such as "great," "gripping," and "riveting."

Roger Ebert, writing in the *Chicago Sun-Times* on January 1, 1976, called it "the most observant study of working journalists we're ever likely to see in a feature film." He added that "it succeeds brilliantly" in showing the mix of highs and lows, fear and courage that propelled Woodward and Bernstein. "There's not a false or 'Hollywood' note in the whole movie."[1]

Director Alan J. Pakula and Dustin Hoffman on the set of *All the President's Men*. Pakula received an Oscar nomination for the movie.

Variety added its kudos. In its January 1, 1976, issue, it called Alan J. Pakula's directing and William Goldman's scriptwriting "ingenious." Robert Redford and Dustin Hoffman as Woodward and Bernstein "excel," Hal Holbrook as Deep Throat was "outstanding," and Jason Robards as Executive Editor Ben Bradlee provided "an excellent characterization."[2]

Vincent Canby of *The New York Times* wrote on April 8, 1976, that the movie was "a spellbinding detective story" and a "riveting screen adaptation" of the book. The strength of the movie, he added, was "the virtually day-to-day record of the way Bernstein and Woodward conducted their investigations."[3]

Even today, the film still carries solid drama and acute characterizations and is able to excite the critics. Jeffrey M. Anderson, writing for *Combustible Celluloid*, states: "the film remains urgently relevant today as a David-and-Goliath story against those who use political office as a means of obtaining personal power and plotting against their fellow man."[4]

And *TV Guide* called it a "landmark movie" that "features a host of fine character portrayals and a compelling climax."[5]

Viewers who saw the movie decades after it first appeared in 1976 offered comments like:

- "a fine political thriller"
- "the script is marvelous"
- "it never gets old, it never wears thin"
- "a cornerstone of modern cinema"
- "will keep you on the edge of your seat"

In 2006, *All the President's Men* was reissued in a two-disc special edition DVD that included two short "making of" documentaries: "Pressure and the Press" and "Telling the Truth About Lies."

Historical Accuracy

Each of the characters portrayed in the movie actually lived, including the reporters and executive members of the editorial staff at the *Washington Post*, as well as those working for the Committee to Re-elect the

The *Washington Post* Newsroom

Though the movie scenes showing the *Washington Post* newsroom appear actual, they are a re-creation. The set builders tried to duplicate as much as they could, down to the blue and orange filing cabinets and the stickers on Ben Bradlee's secretary's desk. They went so far as to collect several tons of actual papers and trash from the *Post*'s desks and wastebaskets and ship it all to Hollywood for the re-creation. The *Post* would not allow cameras inside the actual newsroom because the activity would interfere with daily newspaper operations, but shots of the building entrance, elevators, and the parking lot were actual.[6]

President. Bernstein's trip to Miami to uncover the Kenneth Dahlberg money in Bernard Barker's account is also accurate, but the movie portrays him using a ruse to get in to see the files when, actually, he was invited to look at them. However, the movie was accurate about his long wait before seeing the files. Frank Wills, the Watergate security guard who discovered the taped stairwell door at the Watergate while the burglars were upstairs, played himself in the movie; all other movie characters were played by actors.

Each of the major events in the movie actually happened, including the misreading of source confirmation and the firestorm of criticism leveled at the *Washington Post* for reporting Bob Haldeman as one of

Actors and reporters attend the premiere of *All the President's Men*. From left are Dustin Hoffman, Carl Bernstein, Bob Woodward, and Robert Redford.

those who controlled the slush fund. The chronological order of events is accurate, though Deep Throat's warning to Woodward that his and Bernstein's lives were in danger actually occurred much later than the time period of the movie; it happened several months afterward. The early-morning meeting between Bradlee, Woodward, and Bernstein concerning confirmation by Deep Throat of Haldeman's control of the slush fund and the cover-up does not appear in their book, *All the President's Men*. But Deep Throat did confirm this information.

The Impact and Historical Significance of the Watergate Case

At three minutes past noon on Friday, August 9, 1974, Vice President Gerald Ford took the oath of office as president of the United States, succeeding Richard Nixon. Watergate had forced a president to resign. Fifty men had been convicted of or pled guilty to crimes.[1] The case had turned a spotlight on the seedy side of national politics and had shown that massive amounts of political money along with a thirst for power could entice high government officials to break the law and violate the Constitution.

The idea that the president could act outside the law and the Constitution without answering to Congress or the courts was rejected. Congress had asserted itself through the impeachment process, making it clear that it could remove the president from office. The Supreme Court had asserted itself by its unanimous decision on the tapes, making it clear that it could control what information the president must provide another branch of government.

Checks and Balances

In the years since Watergate, Congress has reinforced its power with respect to the executive branch by the House of Representatives' impeachment of President Bill Clinton in 1998 on two charges (perjury and obstruction of justice) and by the Senate's acquitting him of both charges in 1999. Had the Senate convicted Bill Clinton, he would have been removed from office.

The Supreme Court has also reinforced its power through several decisions that involved limits on what the president can and cannot do. In 2004, for example, the Court said the president could not lock up, indefinitely, foreign and U.S. citizens without allowing them a chance to show their arrests were wrong. This decision came because President George W. Bush had argued that during the so-called "War on Terror" he had the right to act in any way he chose to protect the interests of Americans. The Court said, no, there were limits on what he could and could not do.

New Laws in the Wake of Watergate

Four months after Richard Nixon's resignation, Congress passed the Privacy Act of 1974, which grew out of the illegal wiretapping and investigations by the Plumbers and others. No federal government agency could now disclose records it had on any person without getting the approval of that person first. As Senator Sam Ervin said when introducing the legislation: "If we have learned anything in this last year of Watergate, it is that there must be limits upon what the Government can know about each of its citizens."[2]

In addition, in 1974 Congress amended the 1971 Federal Election Campaign Act to create the Federal Election Commission to oversee all federal elections and to place limits on who could make campaign contributions as well as what and how much could be contributed in any election. It was a response to the unregulated contributions in millions of dollars that flowed into the Committee to Re-elect the President during the 1972 campaign and that financed the burglaries, the hush money payments, and the Watergate cover-up.

Four years later came the Ethics in Government Act, which set up an Office of Independent Counsel, succeeding the Office of the Watergate Special Prosecutor, and authorizing the investigation of wrongdoing in the executive branch, including the offices of the president, vice president, CIA director, and members of the president's cabinet. Approval and removal of the Independent Counsel was left to a panel of three appeals court judges, thus giving the judicial branch a veto over the appointment, something they did not have during the Watergate days.

Since 1978 and up through the Clinton administration (1993–2001), there have been thirteen independent counsel appointments, involving every administration since Nixon's. Some investigations have resulted in criminal convictions, others have concluded no laws had been broken. The Independent Counsel law had been challenged as constituting a "fourth" branch of government (after the executive, legislative, and judicial branches) because the Independent Counsel was answerable to no one and had virtually unlimited powers. But in 1988, the Supreme Court held that the Independent Counsel law, itself, was constitutional. However, not everyone in government liked the law because, sometimes, the investigations were considered too political and unfair. In 1999, Congress decided not to renew it. The U.S. Department of Justice then regained its old power to investigate and try all violations of federal law, even if those violations occurred in the office of the president of the United States.

As for campaign financing, it did not take long for office seekers to come up with new legal ways to obtain political money. Since 1974, there have been several laws passed, the last being the Bipartisan Campaign Reform Act of 2002 (also known as the McCain-Feingold Act), which limited individuals' contributions to one thousand dollars for any single candidate, among other provisions. But no one expects the excesses in campaign spending that highlighted Watergate to disappear completely, no matter what laws are passed. At most, it is hoped that political contributors and candidates will understand the more money they spend on a political campaign, the more the other side will spend, too. It becomes a race that no one can win.

Presidential Power Plays

Even though the move to increase presidential power was curtailed during Watergate and its immediate aftermath, a new push for it has appeared in recent years, mainly under the presidency of George W. Bush (2001–2009). Not long after the tragedy of September 11, 2001, the president secretly issued an executive order allowing the National Security Agency, the U.S. government's top surveillance arm, to eavesdrop on international telephone calls and e-mail of Americans *without first obtaining a warrant*, as the Constitution requires. Claiming that the government needed to move quickly in this time of instant worldwide communications, the president argued that it simply took too long to go to a court and get a warrant before intercepting a communication.

In 2006, a lower court said such activities were in violation of the Constitution and ordered them stopped. But in 2007, the president and some of his allies in Congress pushed through "The Protect America Act" which, in effect, legalized in the future the kind of eavesdropping already done. Whereas before, a special court (called the Foreign Intelligence Surveillance Court) was supposed to issue a warrant before the eavesdropping took place (though the president often ignored the court), now that power was taken away, and the U.S. attorney general and the director of national intelligence—both members of the executive branch—were given the authority.

The push for increased presidential power has not stopped here. Presidents George H. W. Bush, Bill

Clinton, and George W. Bush, whose terms ran from 1989 to 2009, all used the "signing statement" to indicate how they would interpret a law passed by Congress. (This is an official statement issued by the president at the time he signs a bill into law.) Sometimes they would feel the law was unconstitutional and refuse to enforce it, even though questions of constitutionality were for the Supreme Court—and not the president—to decide. Other times, they would disagree with how Congress thought a law should be interpreted, and they would ignore what Congress intended, even though such questions of intent were for Congress—and not the president—to decide. Before George H. W. Bush's presidency, there had only been 75 presidential signing statements issued in more than 185 years of American history. Since 1989, however, that number has jumped up fivefold, with George W. Bush alone responsible for more than 160 of them.

Even though the move to increase presidential power was curtailed during Watergate and its immediate aftermath, a new push for it has appeared in recent years.

The effect of the signing statement is to allow the president to nullify certain laws he disagrees with, even though those laws were passed in constitutional fashion by Congress and/or upheld by the Supreme Court. Signing statements allow the president to do just about whatever he wishes, even though in 2006 the American Bar Association declared that signing statements are "contrary to the rule of law and our constitutional

New president Gerald Ford and his wife, Betty, walk with Pat and Richard Nixon following the president's resignation. His pardon of Nixon is believed to have contributed to Ford's loss in the 1976 election.

separation of powers."[3] But signing statements continue to be used.

Watergate's Legacy

By the time of Richard Nixon's resignation, the term "Watergate" had entered our language as a synonym for official political misconduct. It did not take long for the suffix "-gate" to attach itself to activities that could have dubious political consequences. In President Jimmy Carter's administration (1977–1981), there was "Peanut*gate*," which involved an alleged scandal over Carter's peanut warehouse, and "Billy*gate*," in which Billy Carter, the president's brother, was accused of influence peddling when he registered as an agent for the foreign government of Libya. In the administration of President Ronald Reagan (1981–1989) there was "Iran*gate*," which involved illegal U.S. government sales of arms to Iran with the proceeds going to those attempting to overthrow the legitimate government of Nicaragua. During the time of President Bill Clinton (1999–2001) there was "Travel*gate*," which involved the firing of seven longtime employees of the White House travel office and replacing them with friends of the president. There has been "Korea*gate*," involving "political gifts" in the hundreds of thousands of dollars from Korean businessman Tongsun Park to various congressmen, and "Waste-water*gate*," in which the Environmental Protection Agency went easy on some polluting companies and delayed toxic-waste cleanup. But Water*gate* was the first, and that word—or its last four letters—will long be remembered as standing for government corruption.

Within three years of the Watergate break-in, almost all of those charged in the burglary, the cover-up, the payment of hush money, the obstructions of justice, and the commission of perjury had either pled guilty or been convicted. By August 10, 1975, a year after Richard Nixon resigned, John Dean, John Ehrlichman, Charles Colson, Bob Haldeman, John Mitchell, and Jeb Magruder had all been sentenced for their roles in the Watergate affair. The special prosecutor continued the Watergate investigation for two more years, prosecuting a few lesser figures. But by the time of the 1976 election, all the major players had received their day in court, and for most, their lives would never be the same.

Thirty days after Nixon resigned, new president Gerald Ford issued him a pardon that prevented any further prosecution for his acts and crimes. The pardon incensed the American electorate, who saw Nixon as "getting away" with his actions. In the 1976 presidential election, the pardon played a strong role in Ford's defeat by Jimmy Carter.

As for Richard Nixon, his attitude can be summed up in public comments he made more than ten years after his resignation. What was Watergate's greatest lesson, he was asked?

"Just destroy all the tapes," he responded.[4]

Alfred C. Baldwin: The "listener" who wrote down what he heard from wiretaps in the DNC offices. He turned himself in to prosecutors a month after the burglary.

Bernard L. Barker: One of the Watergate burglars; pled guilty to conspiracy, burglary, and illegal wiretapping and served twelve months in jail.

Carl Bernstein: Reporter for the *Washington Post*, who, along with Bob Woodward, uncovered major stories about White House involvement with Watergate.

Ben Bradlee: Executive editor of the *Washington Post*.

Alexander P. Butterfield: Deputy assistant to the president, in charge of oval office security; disclosed Nixon's taping system during testimony before the Ervin Committee.

Dwight L. Chapin: Appointments secretary to Richard Nixon; set up contacts with Donald Segretti for "dirty tricks" campaign; pled guilty to making false and misleading statements and served eight months in jail.

Charles W. Colson: Special White House counsel to Richard Nixon; pled guilty to obstruction of justice for conspiracy to defame the reputation of Daniel Ellsberg and served seven months in jail.

Archibald Cox: First Watergate special prosecutor.

John W. Dean III: Counsel to the president; managed the cover-up, pled guilty to conspiracy to obstruct justice, and served four months in jail.

John D. Ehrlichman: Nixon's chief domestic policy adviser; convicted of obstruction of justice, conspiracy, and perjury and served eighteen months in jail.

Sam J. Ervin: Democratic senator from North Carolina; chairman of the Senate Watergate Committee.

Virgilio R. González: One of the Watergate burglars; pled guilty to conspiracy, burglary, and illegal wiretapping and served fifteen months in jail.

L. Patrick Gray III: FBI acting director; destroyed the contents of E. Howard Hunt's White House safe, allowed White House counsel to sit in on FBI interviews with Watergate witnesses, and resigned.

Alexander M. Haig: Succeeded H. R. Haldeman as White House chief of staff.

H. R. (Bob) Haldeman: Nixon's chief of staff until he resigned in April 1973; convicted of obstruction of justice, conspiracy, and perjury and served eighteen months in jail.

E. Howard Hunt: Retired CIA officer, White House consultant, member of "Plumbers," one of the Watergate burglars; pled guilty to conspiracy, burglary, and obstruction of justice and served thirty-three months in jail.

Leon Jaworski: The second Watergate prosecutor.

Herbert W. Kalmbach: Nixon's "West Coast" lawyer; raised hush money; paid Donald Segretti for "dirty tricks"; pled guilty to fund-raising irregularities and served six months in jail.

113

Richard G. Kleindienst: Attorney general to whom G. Gordon Liddy confessed CRP involvement in burglary; received a suspended one-month jail sentence in a non-Watergate matter.

G. Gordon Liddy: Counsel to CRP, member of "Plumbers," one of the Watergate and Fielding office burglars; convicted of conspiracy, burglary, and illegal wiretapping and served fifty-two months in jail.

James W. McCord Jr.: Retired CIA security officer; handled security at CRP, left tape on doors at Watergate, planted wiretaps at DNC, wrote letter to judge implicating others in burglary; convicted of conspiracy, burglary, and illegal wiretapping and served four months in jail.

Jeb Stuart Magruder: Deputy director of CRP; pled guilty to obstruction of justice and perjury and served seven months in jail.

Eugenio Rolando Martínez: One of the Watergate and Fielding office burglars; pled guilty to conspiracy, burglary, and illegal wiretapping and served fifteen months in jail.

John N. Mitchell: U.S. attorney general and director of CRP; convicted of obstruction of justice and conspiracy and served nineteen months in jail.

Richard Nixon: President of the United States 1969–1974; motion to impeach him was passed by the House Judiciary Committee, and he resigned from office August 9, 1974.

Lawrence F. O'Brien: Chairman, Democratic National Committee, whose Watergate office was burglarized by the Watergate burglars.

Elliot L. Richardson: U.S. attorney general; appointed Watergate special prosecutor Archibald Cox and resigned when ordered to fire him.

William S. Ruckelshaus: Assistant attorney general and FBI director; resigned when ordered to fire special prosecutor Archibald Cox.

Peter J. Rodino Jr.: Democratic congressman from New Jersey; chairman of the House Judiciary Committee that brought impeachment charges against Richard Nixon.

Donald H. Segretti: Set up "dirty tricks" campaign against Democratic presidential candidates; pled guilty to distributing illegal campaign literature and served four and one-half months in jail.

Earl J. Silbert: Assistant U.S. attorney for District of Columbia; prosecuted the first Watergate case.

John J. Sirica: Chief judge, U.S. District Court for the District of Columbia; presided over the Watergate trial and the Nixon tapes dispute.

Hugh Sloan: Assistant treasurer of CRP; resigned from the committee in 1972 and gave information to Woodward and Bernstein.

Maurice H. Stans: Finance director, CRP; fined $150,000 for campaign finance irregularities.

Frank A. Sturgis: One of the Watergate burglars; pled guilty to conspiracy, burglary, and illegal wiretapping and served thirteen months in jail.

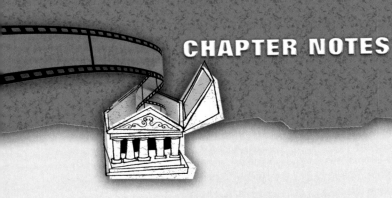

CHAPTER NOTES

 The Letter

1. J. Anthony Lukas, *Nightmare: The Underside of the Nixon Years* (New York: The Viking Press, 1976), p. 218.
2. Ibid., p. 271.
3. John J. Sirica, *To Set the Record Straight* (New York: W. W. Norton & Co., 1979), p. 84.
4. Keith W. Olson, *Watergate: The Presidential Scandal That Shook America* (Lawrence, Kans.: University Press of Kansas, 2003), p. 70.
5. G. Gordon Liddy, *Will, The Autobiography of G. Gordon Liddy* (New York: St. Martin's Press, 1980), p. 406.
6. Sirica, p. 94.
7. Walter Rugaber, "Watergate Spy Says Defendants Were Under 'Political Pressure' To Admit Guilt And Keep Silent," *New York Times*, March 24, 1973, p. 13.
8. Lukas, p. 191.
9. Rugaber.
10. Sirica, p. 95.
11. Ibid., pp. 95–97.
12. Rugaber.

 The Crime

1. J. Anthony Lukas, *Nightmare: The Underside of the Nixon Years* (New York: The Viking Press, 1976), pp. 9–10.
2. Ibid., p. 10.
3. Ibid., p. 11.
4. Fred Emery, *Watergate: The Corruption of American Politics and the Fall of Richard Nixon* (New York: Times Books, 1994), p. 27.
5. Lukas, p. 18.

Chapter Notes

6. Ibid., p. 9.
7. Keith W. Olson, *Watergate: The Presidential Scandal That Shook America* (Lawrence, Kans.: University Press of Kansas, 2003), p. 26.
8. Stanley I. Kutler, *The Wars of Watergate: The Last Crisis of Richard Nixon* (New York: A. A. Knopf, 1990), p. 107.
9. Carl Bernstein and Bob Woodward, *All the President's Men* (New York: Simon & Schuster, 1974), p. 122.
10. Olson, pp. 30–33.
11. Emery, pp. 39–40.
12. Ibid., p. 43.
13. Neil Sheehan, "Vietnam Archive: Pentagon Study Traces 3 Decades of Growing U.S. Involvement," *New York Times*, June 13, 1971, p. 1.
14. Lukas, p. 71.
15. Ibid.
16. Olson, pp. 18–19.
17. Emery, p. 80.
18. Ibid., pp. 89–91.
19. Ibid.
20. Ibid.
21. Ibid., pp. 92–101.
22. Ibid., p. 103.
23. Lukas, pp. 102–103.
24. Ibid., pp. 198–200.
25. Ibid., p. 202.
26. Ibid., p. 204.
27. Olson, p. 45.
28. Emery, p. 133.
29. Ibid., p. 134.
30. Lukas, pp. 206–207.
31. Olson, p. 4.

 3 The Path to Court

1. Carl Bernstein and Bob Woodward, *All the President's Men* (New York: Simon & Schuster, 1974), p. 18.
2. Keith W. Olson, *Watergate: The Presidential Scandal That Shook America* (Lawrence, Kans.: University Press of Kansas, 2003), p. 44.

3. Bernstein and Woodward, p. 20.
4. Ibid., p. 29.
5. J. Anthony Lukas, *Nightmare: The Underside of the Nixon Years* (New York: The Viking Press, 1976), p. 227.
6. Ibid., p. 223.
7. Stanley I. Kutler, ed., *Abuse of Power: The New Nixon Tapes* (New York: The Free Press, 1997), p. 67.
8. Ibid., p. 69.
9. Lukas, p. 234.
10. Ibid.
11. Bernstein and Woodward, p. 73.
12. John D. O'Connor, "I'm the Guy They Called Deep Throat," *Vanity Fair*, July 2005, http://www.vanityfair.com/politics/features/2005/07/deepthroat200507 (June 18, 2006).
13. Bernstein and Woodward, pp. 43–44.
14. Ibid., p. 44.
15. Lukas, p. 250.
16. Ibid., p. 253.
17. Ibid.
18. Ibid., p. 242.
19. Bernstein and Woodward, p. 65.
20. Ibid., p. 73.
21. Ibid.
22. Ibid., p. 69.
23. Ibid., p. 97.
24. Ibid., p. 103.
25. Lukas, p. 274.
26. Bernstein and Woodward, pp. 133–135.
27. Ibid., p. 142.

 The Trial

1. Carl Bernstein and Bob Woodward, *All the President's Men* (New York: Simon & Schuster, 1974), pp. 229–230.
2. Ibid., p. 230.
3. John J. Sirica, *To Set the Record Straight* (New York: W. W. Norton & Co., 1979), p. 64.
4. Ibid., p. 65.
5. J. Anthony Lukas, *Nightmare: The Underside of the Nixon Years* (New York: The Viking Press, 1976), p. 264.

6. Ibid., p. 264.
7. Ibid., p. 267.
8. Ibid., pp. 263–264.
9. Stanley I. Kutler, *The Wars of Watergate: The Last Crisis of Richard Nixon* (New York: The Free Press, 1997), p. 254.
10. Sirica, p. 71.
11. Ibid., p. 74.
12. Ibid., p. 77.
13. Ibid., p. 78.
14. Ibid., p. 84.
15. Ibid., p. 87.

5 The Verdict and Its Consequences

1. John J. Sirica, *To Set the Record Straight* (New York: W. W. Norton & Co., 1979), p. 88.
2. J. Anthony Lukas, *Nightmare: The Underside of the Nixon Years* (New York: The Viking Press, 1976), p. 287.
3. Ibid.
4. Carl Bernstein and Bob Woodward, *All the President's Men* (New York: Simon & Schuster, 1974), p. 273.
5. Fred Emery, *Watergate: The Corruption of American Politics and the Fall of Richard Nixon* (New York: Times Books, 1994), pp. 262–263.
6. Ibid., p. 263.
7. Ibid., pp. 264–265.
8. Ibid., pp. 265–266.
9. Walter Rugaber, "Watergate Spy Says Defendants Were Under 'Political Pressure' To Admit Guilt And Keep Silent," *New York Times*, March 24, 1973, p. 13.
10. Lukas, p. 306.
11. Ibid., p. 308.
12. Ibid., pp. 307–308.
13. Ibid., p. 334.
14. Emery, pp. 337–338.
15. Lukas, p. 338.
16. Ibid., p. 339.
17. Keith W. Olson, *Watergate: The Presidential Scandal That Shook America* (Lawrence, Kans.: University Press of Kansas, 2003), p. 89.

18. Ibid., p. 91.
19. Lukas, pp. 341–342.
20. Olson, p. 98.
21. Lukas, p. 374.
22. Ibid., p. 383.
23. Ibid., p. 393.
24. Ibid., p. 394.
25. Ibid., p. 435.
26. Ibid.
27. Sirica, p. 169.
28. Emery, p. 404.
29. Ibid., p. 406.
30. Stanley I. Kutler, ed., *Abuse of Power: The New Nixon Tapes* (New York: Simon & Schuster, 1998), pp. 252–253.
31. Emery, p. 420.
32. Ibid., p. 410.
33. Ibid., p. 411.
34. Ibid., p. 426.
35. Ibid.
36. Ibid., p. 428.
37. Ibid., p. 429.
38. Ibid., p. 433.
39. Ibid., p. 439.
40. Lukas, p. 513.
41. Emery, p. 448.
42. Ibid., p. 451.
43. Ibid., p. 450.
44. Ibid., p. 459.
45. Lukas, p. 567.

6 The Movie: *All the President's Men*

1. Roger Ebert, movie review, *Chicago Sun-Times*, January 1, 1976, <http://rogerebert.suntimes.com/apps/pbcs.dll/article?AID=/19760101/REVIEWS/601010301/1023> (July 3, 2008).
2. Variety Staff, "All the President's Men," *Variety.com*, January 1, 1976, <http://www.variety.com/VE1117796604.html?categoryid=31&cs=1&p=0> (May 17, 2008).
3. Vincent Canby, movie review, *New York Times*, April 8, 1976, <http://movies.nytimes.com/movie/review?res=9C0DEEDF1

■■■■■■■■■■■■■■■■■■■■■■■■■■■■■■■■■

43BE43ABC4053DFB266838D669EDE&scp=16&sq=movie%20reviews%20archive%20Canby&st=cse> (May 23, 2008).

4. Anderson, Jeffrey M., *The Unmaking of the President*, n.d., <http://www.combustiblecelluloid.com/classic/allpress.shtml> (January 26, 2007).

5. T.V. Guide.com, n.d., <http://www.tvguide.com/movies/presidents-men/review/112343> (May 17, 2008).

6. Matt Slovick, "All the President's Men," n.d., <http://www.google.com/search?q=Matt+Slovick+All+the+President's+Men&ie=UTF-8&oe=UTF-8> (January 26, 2007).

7 The Impact and Historical Significance of the Watergate Case

1. Vic Ratner, "WATERGATE PROSECUTION REPORT," October 15, 1975, <http://openweb.tvnews.vanderbilt.edu/1975-10/1975-10-15-ABC-2.html> (February 2, 2007).

2. *Legislative History of the Privacy Act of 1974, S. 3418* (Public law 93-579), Committee on Government Operations, United States Senate and the Committee on Government Relations, House of Representatives, Subcommittee on Government Information and Individual Rights, September 1976, p. 4, <http://www.loc.gov/rr/frd/Military_Law/pdf/LH_privacy_act-1974.pdf.> (July 7, 2008).

3. James Bovard, "Bush's Signing Statement Dictatorship," *The Future of Freedom Foundation Commentaries*, October 9, 2006, <http://www.fff.org/comment/com0610c.asp> (May 21, 2008).

4. Stanley I. Kutler, *The Wars of Watergate: The Last Crisis of Richard Nixon* (New York: The Free Press, 1997), p. 616.

GLOSSARY

abuse of power—One of the impeachment charges against Richard Nixon. Generally, it occurs when someone in authority takes action or persuades others to take action that he or they are not authorized to take.

bail—Money paid by someone charged or convicted of a crime in order to remain, temporarily, free from jail. The judge decides the amount of bail.

burglary—A crime where there has been a break-in for the purpose of committing another crime (such as illegal wiretapping) inside the building.

CIA (Central Intelligence Agency)—The nation's largest spy organization, responsible for collecting foreign intelligence from around the world and carrying out covert activity.

closed session—A meeting from which the public and the press are excluded.

conspiracy—A crime in which two or more people agree to break the law and then attempt to carry it out. The crime of conspiracy is the agreement to break the law, not the actual commission of the criminal act.

contempt of Congress—The refusal of U.S. government officials or private citizens to appear and testify before a U.S. congressional committee after receiving a congressional subpoena to do so.

covert activity—Secret work performed by an agent of a U.S. security service (such as CIA or FBI) operating on behalf of the U.S. government under a false identity and/or disguising for whom he or she works.

CRP—The Committee to Re-elect the President, established to run the reelection campaign of Richard Nixon in 1972.

executive clemency—A pardon issued by the president for a criminal act.

FBI (Federal Bureau of Investigation)—The chief law enforcement arm of the U.S. government.

impeach—To charge a public official with crimes while in office. A hearing on the charges is then held to decide whether they are true. The right to impeach the president is set forth in the U.S. Constitution (Article II, Section 4, for "treason, bribery or other high crimes and misdemeanors") with the House of Representatives having the sole right to bring the charges and the Senate the sole right to decide whether the charges are true.

indict—To officially charge with a crime.

obstruction of justice—A crime in which there is interference with the normal process of law enforcement.

Pentagon Papers—An in-depth study of U.S. involvement in Vietnam, containing graphic portrayal of secret bombings, attacks, and casualties, most of which had not been shared with the American people. Portions of the study were photocopied by Daniel Ellsberg, published in *The New York Times* and *Washington Post* in June 1971.

perjury—The crime of lying under oath.

Plumbers—A group of White House aides who worked to stop "leaks" of information to the press.

subpoena—A written command issued by a court or congressional committee for a person to appear and give testimony.

unindicted coconspirator—Someone whom the grand jury believes joined a conspiracy to break the law but who will not be indicted because of insufficient proof.

wiretapping—Installation of electronic devices in telephones or on telephone or telegraph wires for the purpose of intercepting conversations. Such activity is a crime unless done by federal or state law enforcement personnel with an approved warrant.

Books

Anderson, Dale. *Watergate: Scandal in the White House.* Minneapolis: Compass Point Books, 2007.

Gold, Susan Dudley. *The Pentagon Papers: National Security or the Right to Know.* New York: Benchmark Books, 2004.

McConnell, William S., editor. *Watergate.* Farmington Hills, Mich.: Greenhave Press/Thomson Gale, 2006.

Schuman, Michael A. *Richard Nixon* (revised edition). Berkeley Heights, N.J.: Enslow Publishers, Inc., 2003.

Tracey, Kathleen. *The Watergate Scandal.* Hockesson, Del.: Mitchell Lane Publishing, 2006.

Van Meter, Larry A. *United States v. Nixon. The Question of Executive Privilege.* New York: Chelsea House, 2007.

Internet Addresses

Richard M. Nixon: The Watergate Tapes
<http://www.lib.berkeley.edu/MRC/watergate.html>

Richard Nixon Library and Birthplace Foundation
<http://www.nixonfoundation.org>

Woodward and Bernstein Watergate Papers
<http://www.hrc.utexas.edu/research/fn/woodstein.series.html>

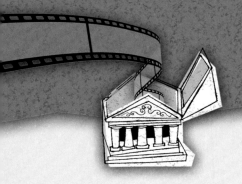

INDEX